kids who laugh

How to Develop Your Child's Sense of Humor

Louis R. Franzini, PhD

SQUAREONE
PUBLISHERS

Cover Designer: Phaedra Mastrocola
Typesetter: Gary A. Rosenberg
Editor: Carola Roseby

Square One Publishers
Garden City Park, NY 11040
(516) 535-2010
www.squareonepublishers.com

The photo on page 135 originally appeared in the *East County Californian*, and has been reprinted with the permission of Ion Moe.

Library of Congress Cataloging-in-Publication Data

Franzini, Louis R., 1941–
    Kids who laugh : how to develop your child's sense of humor / Louis R. Franzini.
        p. cm.
Includes bibliographical references (p.   ) and index.
    ISBN 0-7570-0008-8
    1. Humor in children. 2. Child rearing. I. Title.
    BF723.H85 .F73 2002
    155.4'18—dc21

                                                            2001006937

Printed in the United States of America

10   9   8   7   6   5   4   3   2   1

Contents

Acknowledgments, vii

A Word About Gender, ix

Introduction, 1

1. All About Humor, 5

2. Characteristics of Children's Humor, 21

3. Play, Smiles, and Laughter, 37

4. Developing Your Child's Humor Skills, 51

5. Encouraging Your Child to Create Humor, 65

6. Potential Abuses of Humor by Children, 85

7. Humor Use by Special Needs Children, 103

8. Jest for Teachers (& Parents, Too), 117

9. Using Humor Resources, 137

Conclusion, 161

References, 163

Suggested Readings, 167

Suggested Websites, 169

Index, 171

This book is dedicated to my son Sam,
now age one, who has become a living laboratory
for many of my words in Kids Who Laugh.

He laughs a lot and loves unconditionally.
He is a treasure far beyond his parents' dreams.

Acknowledgments

I am very appreciative of the many helpful suggestions and contributions made by editor Carola Roseby and publisher Rudy Shur. My beautiful, loving wife, Jessica, was most helpful in reviewing the manuscript, offering suggestions, giving me the time to write, and occasionally reminding me of the importance of keeping my own sense of humor intact. Of course, our happy son Sam served as a daily inspiration to my writing. I am very pleased to share our joy from him with my readers. Finally, I appreciate the ongoing interest in and support of this project by Jeremy and Stacy Franzini and all the parents and kids whose photos are included.

A Word About Gender

To avoid long and awkward phrasing within sentences, the publisher has chosen to alternate the use of male and female pronouns according to chapter. Therefore, when referring to your child, odd-numbered chapters use male pronouns, while even-numbered chapters employ female pronouns, to give acknowledgment to children of both genders.

Introduction

A GOOD SENSE OF HUMOR IS ONE of the most desirable personality characteristics a person can develop. A sense of humor can be honed to become a personal asset that lasts a lifetime. It is the quality we seek most often in our friends, our mates, and our children. Funny people are enjoyable to be around and become the preferred companions of people of all ages.

Parents want their children to be healthy and happy. Conscientious expectant mothers take their prenatal vitamins faithfully every day to ensure the health of their babies. After birth, caring parents diligently provide for their children's physical needs. They cover outlets with plastic safety caps and place gates across stairways. They serve nutritious meals. They schedule regular pediatric checkups. They enroll their children in ballet classes, gymnastics, Little League, and the like so that they can stay in good physical shape. The list of things that parents do for their children to ensure that they grow up healthy goes on and on. What they don't do, in far too many cases, is seek out specific learning experiences that will promote their children's personal happiness, such as helping them to develop a good sense of humor.

Many parents do not realize that they can help their children develop a sense of humor. They think it's all a matter of chance. But, luckily, it's not. There is conclusive evidence that children's appreciation and use of humor are learned. In fact, humor development begins with parents' early attempts to coax smiles out of their newborns. Unfortunately, most people have no idea how to continue this process as their children grow so that they can eventually create humor and use it socially in positive ways. Fortunately, there are specific techniques and strategies that you can apply to nurture your child's sense of humor—whether your child is an infant, a toddler, one who has just started school, or a preteen.

Why should you make a conscious effort to promote this quality in your child? Because a well-developed sense of humor is a genuine asset to any child and helps ensure a strong, positive self-image. A child who enjoys and remembers a joke or riddle and passes it on to others feels an enormous personal accomplishment and establishes friendships at the same time. Making others laugh is extremely rewarding to children (as it is to all of us).

Humor can also be used as a coping device to help children overcome shyness or being teased. Rather than fighting—or retreating into a shell—a child with a well-developed sense of humor is more likely to gain acceptance and make friends. Kids with problems, such as a speech defect or a physical handicap, can make special use of their humor skills to be genuinely accepted by their peers. Robin Williams, Jay Leno, Molly Shannon, and many other professional comedians credit their ability to cope with the stresses of growing up or being seen as "different" to a good sense of humor.

Kids Who Laugh is not intended to train future show biz comics, however. It is designed to introduce the many positive effects a well-developed sense of humor has on children and to teach you how to help your child cultivate this desirable characteristic. *Kids Who Laugh* is all about showing kids how to have fun by enjoying the humor of others, and it's about helping kids enjoy the process of creating humor for themselves and for their friends and families. This is not a joke book or a collection of funny stories for you to read to your child. In fact, it will not necessarily be a very funny book to read (although that's hard for me to admit). In this book, drawing on my expertise and experience as a clinical psychologist and father of three, I tell you what to do to encourage the development of a sense of humor in your child, how to do it, and where to get help. I discuss specific family games, improvisational exercises, resources, and more, which enable both you and your child to practice and hone your humor skills.

Chapter 1 of *Kids Who Laugh* provides you with an overview of humor. It describes the great nature versus nurture debate— are we born with a sense of humor or can it be learned? Then it goes on to discuss what a sense of humor is and the qualities of a humorous outlook, and briefly touches upon some theories of humor. Most important, it discusses the many advantages of a good sense of humor in kids. Chapter 2 describes the categories of children's humor and age-related stages of humor development, and winds up with a discussion of the use of humor in children's literature, television, and movies.

Chapter 3 of *Kids Who Laugh* discusses play, smiles, and laughter and their respective roles in children's humor, and covers the many benefits of laughter on the body. In Chapter 4, you'll learn how to go about developing your child's humor appreciation skills—lowering social barriers, demonstrating your own appreciation of humor, and much more. Then in Chapter 5 comes the really fun stuff: humor-creation exercises. You and your child are sure to experience a lot of laughs while participating in these suggested activities. Chapter 6 covers a more serious topic—the potential abuses of humor by children, such as laughing at others and their mistakes, and how that can be hurtful and damaging to relationships.

Chapter 7 of *Kids Who Laugh* discusses the role of humor in and with special needs children, specifically how humor can help such children cope with a world that can sometimes be intolerant. If you're a teacher who would like to encourage kids' humor in your classroom, Chapter 8 is for you. It includes classroom activities that you can organize to help promote the use of humor by your students. (This chapter contains some useful information for parents, too!) Finally, Chapter 9 identifies helpful humor resources—which are more numerous than you might think—and provides you with criteria you can use to judge these resources.

The main goal of *Kids Who Laugh* is to promote the development of a sense of humor in children, which, in turn, will serve them well throughout their lives. Truly happy people enjoy the journey through life, including some unexpected trips along life's inevitable and numerous detours. "Kids who laugh" are fun to be with and have lots of fun themselves. It's safe to conclude that these are also happy kids who will grow into kind and lighthearted adults. I hope that you will use the guidelines and techniques presented in *Kids Who Laugh* to make living with your child the great fun that it should be.

CHAPTER 1

All About Humor

A sense of humor is just common sense dancing.

—CLIVE JAMES, AUSTRALIAN NOVELIST AND POET
AND BRITISH TV HOST

THE KEY TO UNDERSTANDING HUMOR is to realize that it is simply an enigma wrapped in a conundrum, disguised as a puzzle. What could be clearer than that? Here, I intend to unwrap it and expose it. Later on, I'll help you develop a healthy sense of humor in your child. This chapter first covers the great debate over whether a child's sense of humor is inborn or whether it can be developed through training and experiences in a humor-rich environment. It then discusses what humor is and what we mean by a sense of humor. Next, it briefly reviews a few of the major theories of humor that philosophers and psychologists have developed over the last few hundred years. The chapter then quickly explores the differences in humor appreciation between the two genders and, finally, it reviews the many advantages that kids will enjoy when they have a good sense of humor. So, let's begin.

THE GREAT NATURE VS. NURTURE DEBATE

Is a child's sense of humor an innate trait or is it learned? Can it be enhanced by relevant experiences? These are just a couple of the fundamental "nature versus nurture" questions about basic human characteristics that have been debated for centuries. Those who favor the "nature" position believe that most human behavioral characteristics are due to our inherited genetic traits, that is, what our parents have passed on to us biologically. Those who favor the "nurture" position agree that most of our physical characteristics are due to our biological inheritances, but our psychological characteristics such as personality, temperament, and sense of humor arise from our unique learning experiences from birth onward.

One of the best scientific methods used to sort out the question of nature versus nurture is research conducted on twins. This type of study allows scientists to calculate the relative degrees of influence that genetics and environment have on a particular behavior or human characteristic. Our special interest, of course, is in the personality characteristic of sense of humor. In this model, researchers compare the responses of laughter or funniness ratings to the same humor stimuli by pairs of identical twins (those who share 100 percent of their genes) and fraternal twins (those who share on average 50 percent of their genes).

Lynn Cherkas and colleagues at St. Thomas' Hospital in London used this sound twin research model to determine whether a person's sense of humor is influenced more by genetics or more by environmental experiences. To do so, they presented a series of Gary Larson's *The Far Side* cartoons to 127 pairs of twins. These particular cartoons were chosen because it was observed that *The Far Side* series tends to produce a wide range of responses, from hysterical laughter to no reaction at all.

In this study, the twins (some identical, some fraternal) ranged in age from twenty to seventy-five. Placed in separate rooms, each twin rated the funniness of five *Far Side* cartoons. If the identical twins' ratings were more similar to each other than those of the fraternal twins, it could be reasonably concluded that their senses of humor had been more influenced by genetics (nature) than by the environment (nurture).

Interestingly, this research team had expected to discover that genetics plays a significant role in determining an individual's sense of humor. Thus, the team was quite surprised by its findings: The correlations of the identical twins' funniness ratings of the five cartoons were not greater than those of the fraternal twins. The Cherkas research team thereby credited the twins' upbringing, or their *shared environment,* as the critical determining factor in developing their senses of humor. ("Shared environment" refers to the twins' experiences within their family, influences from peers, and formal education.) The researchers rather reluctantly concluded that the appreciation of the cognitive forms of humor, as uniquely displayed in Larson's cartoons, show "no significant contribution from genetic factors." I heartily agree and proclaim that a child's sense of humor does indeed come primarily from Mom and Dad, but not from their eggs and sperm! My position in the great nature versus nurture debate is this: *No one is born with a great sense of humor, a poor sense of humor, or even no sense of humor.*

Clearly, a sense of humor is *learned,* just like most other skills we possess—riding a bike, swimming the backstroke, being polite, or learning to write. Just because most sixty-five-year-olds cannot surf the Internet and most six-year-olds can do so with ease does not mean that, due to some random electronic mutations, kids in the twenty-first century are born possessing full computer literacy. Kids simply acquire those skills very early in life at school and at home. And they can acquire humor-making and humor-appreciating skills the same way.

Parents are the most important influences on their children's personalities. Whatever genetic factors potentially influence the personality equation have already been contributed at the critical moment of conception. From that point on, it is too late to offer any new and insightful recommendations on how to conceive a humorous child. All of the environmental influences on the new-born child can now begin.

Comic playwright Neil Simon once confessed, "No one has yet determined, to my satisfaction, what elements of nature, genetics, and environment have to combine to form a man or woman with a keen sense of humor. . . . Poverty and bigotry, plus at least a half-dozen factors more, might start to explain where the comic spirit is born. In my case you would certainly have to add 'encouragement.'" Life experiences are clearly very important in developing a child's humorous outlook on life. When a child's humor development is "encouraged," to use Simon's term—that is, praised and appreciated by the world—it will flourish.

Now that we know that humor is part of the nurturing process, let's look at how humor and a sense of humor are defined.

WHAT EXACTLY IS HUMOR AND A SENSE OF HUMOR?

Let's start by defining humor in a very general sense: Humor is the quality that makes something funny. As for the sense of humor, we might think of it as our sixth sense. A sense of humor can be just as useful as the other five senses—seeing, hearing, tasting, touching, and smelling. We cannot assume that someone who doesn't think a particular joke is funny lacks this sixth sense. It's important to understand that people with a well-developed sense of humor differ in the kinds of humor they enjoy. Some children (and adults) think that clowns are funny, while some people find nothing funny about them. Is a cream pie smashed in the face funny? Yes? What if it happened to you? Maybe then it wouldn't be so funny. And what happens if you get angry with the person who smashed the pie in your face? There's a very good chance you'll be accused of having no sense of humor!

Perhaps we should be more explicit about the term "sense of humor." Of course, theorists have offered many formal and complicated definitions. Researchers in humor have produced many technical descriptions of the sense of humor in terms of test-score profiles, self-definitions, and ratings of predetermined humor stimuli, such as cartoons and jokes. Most of these definitions will not be of much use to us because our concern in this book is more practical: how to develop a sense of humor in children. For our purposes, a "sense of humor" is simply a person's propensity for being amused and amusing others. That amusement may or may not result in overt laughter.

Although the foregoing definition should be enough to get you started, the work of personality researchers Willibald Ruch and Franz-Josef Hehl may help you to better recognize and develop the different aspects of your child's sense of humor. Hehl and Ruch subdivided the overall concept of a sense of humor into four facets, or aspects. Each facet may serve as a separate goal for you in your humor-development exercises with your child.

The first facet of the sense of humor, according to Ruch and Hehl, is called *comprehension*. Comprehension refers to how we see and understand humor stimuli. When a comedian tells a joke or a friend poses a riddle, does the child "get" it? Is the short story of the joke understood as something funny, or at least as having been intended to be funny?

The researchers refer to the second facet of humor as *appreciation*, that is, does the child actually experience the humor message as humorous? Is that humor stimulus, be it a funny story, cartoon, or clown, enjoyed?

The third facet of the sense of humor is *expression*, which refers to the quality and quantity of a reaction to the humor stimuli. Most people will credit someone with a "great" sense of humor simply if that person laughs loudly and frequently. Do we understand, appreciate, and enjoy the joke, but show no outward indication that we do? Or do we merely smile in response? In fact, the possible range of reactions could extend from no overt response whatsoever to some chuckling all the way to loud and hearty laughter to the point of tears, side aches, and literally falling down. Prolonged strong laughter can actually weaken your knees.

Finally, Ruch and Hehl include *creation* of humor as the fourth facet, and an important one at that. Humor making involves changing neutral stimuli (events, observations, or words) into funny stimuli. Producing humor can be a rather difficult assignment requiring intelligence, creativity, and sensitivity to various social concerns about the appropriateness of the humor.

As with any other ability, not all children will be equally good at each of these facets. That is fine and expected. It is certainly easier for most people to comprehend and appreciate humor than to create it. That is why audiences easily outnumber comedy writers and performers. It is best to follow your child's lead and note what he enjoys most within the overall realm of humor, in terms of these four facets and the specific types and content of his most preferred humor.

THE QUALITIES OF
A HUMOROUS PERSPECTIVE ON LIFE

A child with a well-developed sense of humor will have acquired a humorous perspective on life—that is, the child will have become a joy tracker or humor spotter in everyday life. Humor is shown in many ways beyond the repetition of rehearsed jokes and riddles. It eventually becomes a frame of mind, a point of view in the child—a point of view that will be carried into adulthood.

According to clinical psychologist Harvey Mindess, there are six specific qualities of a humorous perspective: flexibility, spontaneity, unconventionality, shrewdness, playfulness, and humility. Dr. Mindess has written about the characteristics of humor and has advocated its use in the practice of psychotherapy for over three decades. We can benefit from his knowledge. Let's take a close look at these six qualities with some illustrative examples.

1. Flexibility—a cognitive ability to examine things from different sides other than the most obvious. Double-meaning words are keys to funniness in verbal humor, especially puns—the humorous use of alternate word meanings and sounds. *"How did Samson die? From fallen arches."* Flexibility can be a key to visual humor, too. For example, sticking a banana in your ear or talking to your shoe as if it were a telephone requires a cognitive shift to a different and silly way to use these items.

2. Spontaneity—the ability to move instantly and unpredictably from one mood or form of thinking to another. It is impossible to teach or command spontaneity, of course, but this quality will follow as your child becomes more comfortable and skilled in the use of verbal humor. For example, when something unexpected happens (something you can't prepare for),

Forms of Humor

In general, humor appears in three forms—verbal, written, and visual—either singularly or in any combination. Within these three forms fall all different types of humor—from absurdity to double meanings to exaggeration to wit. These types of humor can be presented or expressed in any number of ways—through actions, comedies, joke-telling, playful conversation, stories, and so on. There are scores of different (and often overlapping) types, sub-types, and expressions of humor. In fact, to cover them all would take a book and a half!

Children and adults may appreciate the same expressions of humor—jokes, for example—but what you should understand is that it is often the subject of the humor and the way it is presented that will strike people of different intellectual levels and experiences as funny. In general, the subjects of the humor that adults enjoy are often too sophisticated or are expressed in a too subtle or complex manner to be appreciated by kids, whose cognitive and intellectual development and base of general knowledge are not yet sufficiently advanced. For example, many adults tend to enjoy jokes with a sexual theme. In most cases, though, a preteen child who overhears such a joke won't understand the punch line because it is beyond the scope of his experience. In many cases, even if kids do understand the humorous message being relayed, the subjects that adult humorists and audiences enjoy are often inappropriate for children.

We should encourage children to enjoy humor in all its forms, while keeping in mind that certain subjects and expressions of humor are still beyond their scope of understanding or maturity level. Once you read Chapter 2, which specifically addresses the categories of humor that children generally enjoy and comprehend, you'll be better prepared to distinguish between adult humor and humor that your child can appreciate and create.

such as a sudden loud noise, spontaneous humor would be to say something like, *"Was that the stock market falling?"* Or *"Did a rich lady drop the stone from her ring?"*

3. Unconventionality—the ability to get beyond the standard most widely accepted values and norms of the culture. Humor relies on identifying the unexpected and often the unaccepted social behaviors or verbal comments. That is why children's unabashedly blunt comments are funny, when the same words from an adult would be socially unacceptable. Comedian Steven Wright's anecdote reflects the humorous quality of unconventionality: *"I was sad because I had no shoes, until I met a man who had no feet. So I said, 'Got any shoes you're not using?'"*

4. Shrewdness—the refusal to believe that anyone, including yourself, really is what he or she seems to be. For example, comedian Roseanne claims that her kids love her because she is like the mother they never had. The humor maker is the first to acknowledge that all of us are pretenders in one way or another. We may mask our fears with humor, and we may make fun of our own shortcomings: *"I'm laughing at your mistakes because I've done the same dumb things."*

5. Playfulness—seeing life as a game to be played for fun and not as a contest to be won. The real purpose of life is enjoyment, not achievement of money or possessions. The winner is *not* the one who dies with the most toys; it is the one who has lived life with the greatest of joy. He who laughs lasts.

6. Humility—the ability not to take oneself too seriously and to recognize the meaninglessness of even your most profound thoughts. Those who express their sense of humor are always taking some risk—of appearing foolish, of not being taken seriously under any circumstances, of being laughed at rather

than laughed with. But the rewards of laughter and closer personal relationships are so great and so probable that they are definitely worth the social risks.

Based on his long career of applying humor in his therapy practice, Dr. Mindess has provided us with a helpful cluster of personal qualities that he has found to contribute to a person's sense of humor. He regards our sense of the ridiculous as an antidote to emotional distress and "a coping mechanism of the very highest caliber." These six qualities become a part of a person's overall humorous attitude and outlook on life. In some ways, these characteristics sound like the very opposite of what society traditionally promotes as desirable traits in the mature and responsible adult. The spontaneous, the unconventional, the playful person really is not very much like the stereotypical sober and serious citizen who is "all business." Which of these role models will you choose for your child? Which kind of person would you yourself most enjoy being with?

THEORIES OF HUMOR

The scientific study of humor has been likened to dissecting a frog to understand how it lives and functions. In the process, both humor and the frog are destroyed. We will try very hard to avoid that outcome here. We're only going to cover a few theories of humor, but believe it or not, there are more than one hundred separate theories of humor. Some are quite elaborate, and some consist of just a few sentences describing one type of humor. Some are merely various philosophers' musings on humor and comedy as unique qualities to be found only in human animals. Other theories are more complex, truly esoteric, and not fun to read.

The three most widely accepted theories by current humor researchers are the *Superiority Theory*, the *Relief From Tension Theory*, and the *Incongruity Theory*, each of which is discussed in some relatively painless detail below. Following that, we'll take a very quick look at some other theories of humor.

The Superiority Theory

The Superiority Theory suggests that situations or comments become humorous to us because we end up feeling better about ourselves when some misfortune or degradation happens to others. That is why it seems funny when we see a pompous man slip and fall on a banana peel—it is happening to someone else. We are not adversely affected because we are in the superior position. Of course, it would *not* be funny if the person falling were a frail elderly gentleman. Another aspect of the Superiority Theory is that children will laugh at any evidence that they have grown up a bit and are now unlike the younger child in a story or movie who makes foolish mistakes or gets confused or acts silly. They end up feeling superior to their younger selves.

The Relief From Tension Theory

This theory, described in detail first by Sigmund Freud, suggests that humor results when a joke or witty comment serves to release our pent-up sexual or aggressive tensions. Humor provides a socially acceptable and safe outlet for those biologically based drives that are present in all of us. That is why so many jokes have hostile or sexual themes. These kinds of jokes are also the ones most likely to be deemed socially offensive, which Freud explains by their ability to trigger psychologically defensive reactions in some especially sensitive listeners.

The Incongruity Theory

Humor, according to the Incongruity Theory, arises when there are unexpected outcomes in familiar circumstances. A person may suddenly look or act in such a way that is unexpected or different from the norm. For example, if Mom returns from the hairdresser with a radically different hairstyle or color, baby may be surprised and smile. An older child might just burst out laughing. If a solid object like a car suddenly collapses, it is funny to young children because their expectations have been violated. When weak figures in a story, such as a child or small animal, outwit or overpower adults or larger animals, the anti-authority result becomes funny to children. (Incongruity as a characteristic of children's humor is discussed in Chapter 2.)

Other Theories of Humor

Philosophers from ancient times up through contemporary communication experts and social psychologists have been presenting their own special theories of humor. This discussion includes a brief description of the humor theories of John Morreall, Charles Gruner, and Sigmund Freud because each highlights a facet of humor not featured in the "Big Three" theories that were discussed above.

Humor theorist John Morreall's view is that humor results from a person's experience of a sudden and pleasant psychological shift. The punch line strikes him in a way that was not predictable, thereby producing enjoyment. "Getting" a joke requires mental effort and feels good emotionally.

Humor theorist Charles Gruner's theory is based on the notion of winning and losing. Simply put, for him "laughter equals winning." He prefers to interpret all humorous situations (events, jokes, riddles, and so on) as a matter of someone gaining something and someone else losing something. As in most of life's contests, it is better to win. And more fun! Gruner is one of the few theorists who argue that their view can explain *all* instances and forms of humor.

Many people are not aware that Sigmund Freud gave considerable attention to the role of humor in an individual's personality. He even told jokes to his patients during their therapy sessions. He also wrote a significant amount about wit and humor—although nearly nothing about humor in children. However, he did theorize that children move through three separate stages in the development of joking. The first stage is *play,* which features incongruous or absurd objects, words, or ideas. He called the second stage *jesting,* during which the child attempts to make the absurdities more meaningful. Finally, Freud described the *joke façade,* which means that the true sexual or aggressive nature of the jokes is disguised. The jokes represent ways that these impulses can get gratified without actually engaging in the behaviors of sex or aggression. (With Freud, it always seems to come back to that.)

Knowing the details of any of the major theories of humor most likely will *not* automatically make you a funny person or, for that matter, a better teacher of humor. But it may reassure you to know that humor has, indeed, long been an important topic to philosophers and researchers, and remains crucial to your child's personal growth.

DOES GENDER MATTER?

Developing your child's sense of humor is important whether your child is a boy or a girl, and it does not matter whether you are a mom or a dad. Everyone can help and everyone can benefit. Yes, there do seem to be certain differences between male and female adults in their senses of humor. For example, men tend to favor sexual humor and women tend to enjoy relationship humor. Interestingly, the gap is narrowing regarding sexual humor, perhaps due to the increasing "liberation" of women who may now feel freer to admit their true tastes. Feminists (of both genders) express great enjoyment of feminist humor in which men are demeaned. This latter finding from research literature is a bit surprising, but it could be one way men try to curry favor with women: *"I'm just like you."*

Similarly, there are differences between men and women in whether they are likely to initiate humorous comments in public settings. Men are more likely to make jokes in general, and are comfortable doing so in mixed groups. Women are more comfortable initiating humor in same-sex groups. These particular issues, though, are less relevant to developing a sense of humor in kids. We encourage *all* parents to promote humor in *all* their children. For once, gender does not matter.

THE ADVANTAGES OF A GOOD SENSE OF HUMOR IN KIDS

Why take on the task of helping your child develop his sense of humor? For all the great benefits, of course! Let's look at the ten main advantages of a well-developed sense of humor in children, which are certain to enhance your understanding of how important this quality can be.

1. Kids who are able to laugh at the funny side of life can be described as "internally happy." It is reasonable to assume that such kids are less vulnerable to assorted adult traumas of poor self-esteem, which can result in excessive shyness or depressive episodes.

2. Psychological research has linked a keen sense of humor in children to a greater degree of intelligence, more extensive creative abilities, more flexible thought processes, greater sociability, higher self-esteem, better-developed self-control skills, and many other attractive personality traits.

3. Kids who have a sense of humor exhibit other desirable emotions, such as a concern for others and their feelings, love displayed through jesting, and a preference for social inclusion rather than exclusion.

4. Kids with a good sense of humor tend to be well liked by their peers, their siblings, their parents, and other adults who get to know them.

5. A humorous perspective increases a child's overall enjoyment of life and day-to-day experiences.

6. A sense of humor can help children cope with both environmental and physical stressors and may even increase their lifespan by reducing susceptibility to minor illnesses and even major diseases. Interestingly, centenarians (people who live to 100 years old or older) typically cite their sense of humor as a major contributor to their longevity.

7. The use of humor can help children cope with a whole variety of adverse circumstances that are typical of a youngster's life: confrontations with schoolyard bullies; dealing with potentially embarrassing situations, such as spilling soda on themselves and being teased by other kids for wetting their pants; finding themselves in new and difficult social situations; and so on.

8. Kids who have a well-developed sense of humor make their parents feel good. One of the most rewarding events for parents, or any adult, is to hear a happy child laugh.

9. Kids with a good sense of humor help society by being joyful citizens. A humor-filled child is an asset in the family, in the classroom, and in the neighborhood.

10. A sense of humor is especially relevant when kids grow up and choose their life partners. Interviews with long-married couples quite often reveal that a sense of humor in each spouse is one of the keys to a successful marriage.

As you can see, there are many advantages to having a good sense of humor—the most outstanding of which is being a happy person in general. This quality will be with your child as he grows and enters adulthood. Get ready to help your child take advantage of the funny side of life—and everyone will benefit.

CONCLUSION

In this chapter, you learned that a sense of humor is influenced by early life experiences and that you play a very important role in developing this quality in your child. I have given you a look at humor in general, and have defined what a sense of humor means to us. I've even covered some theories of humor. But most important, I've explained why a sense of humor is so beneficial for lifelong happiness. Now, what should you know about the categories of children's humor and the stages of humor development? How can you apply that information to promote greater use and appreciation of humor in your child? The following chapter should help you on your way.

CHAPTER 2

Characteristics of Children's Humor

The forbidden is always funny.
The funniest word in the vocabulary
of a second grader is "underwear."

—BETSY BYARS,
AUTHOR OF CHILDREN'S BOOKS

ADULTS USUALLY DON'T THINK the word "underwear" by it-self is that funny; they only care that it's clean. Our ideas of what's humorous will usually be quite different from our children's—and rightly so! Children themselves vary in what they consider funny, depending on their degree of mental development or just on their personal preferences.

There is actually a great diversity in the humor that kids pre-fer. There are several categories of children's humor, which can take many possible forms—jokes and riddles, slapstick, verbal silliness, mockery and ridicule, and so on. In this chapter, I will define and discuss each of these categories and provide you with some guidelines as to when and how humor of various types emerges and develops in children.

CATEGORIES OF CHILDREN'S HUMOR

In Chapter 1, you learned that some types of humor are too sophisticated to be appreciated by children. So let's get back to kids and discuss the categories of humor that children enjoy. Of course, there are dozens and dozens of types of humor, so the categories that follow represent only the most common forms.

Absurdity

Absurdity includes statements, behaviors, or objects that are perceived as ridiculous, irrational, or nonsensical because they are inconsistent with known truths. For example, a boy loses his favorite toy in the backyard but spends his time looking for it in the bedroom because the light is so much better there. (How absurd!)

Defiance

Defiance is the expression of hostility via rebellion against authority and other conventions of society—such as being responsible, mature, or respectful. Defiant humor is any type of humor that purposely goes against what is socially acceptable. An example would be defying anti-graffiti laws by spray-painting humorous signs on public walls, such as "Ignore this sign!"

Exaggeration

Exaggeration is obviously overstating or understating facts, feelings, experiences, or qualities, such as size or amount. For example, when Paul Bunyan (a giant lumberjack from American folklore) was born, it reportedly took five giant storks working overtime to deliver him.

Human Predicaments

Humorous human predicaments are non-hostile situations in which a person looks foolish or is somehow defeated, leaving the observer feeling superior. For example, consider the self-important guest who attends a summertime party and keeps her nose so high in the air that she tumbles, fully clothed, into her host's swimming pool.

Incongruity

Incongruity involves bringing together two items, people, or ideas that are ordinarily regarded as incompatible. Whatever deviates from the norm usually becomes humorous. For example, a boy goes into a local ice-cream store and orders a slice of pepperoni pizza. A more simplistic form would be a person holding a bedroom slipper against her ear as if it were a telephone.

Mockery and Ridicule

Mockery and ridicule of others or oneself can be either playful or negative and hostile. Playful mockery might involve a child's mimicking Mom's seemingly excessive concern for cleanliness by running dishes into the kitchen to be washed the instant that the last bite of food has been consumed. A more hostile and hurtful example of ridicule could involve a child's stuttering in front of another child who has such a speech problem. This type of negative humor appeals to children perhaps because it makes them feel superior to the victims of the jokes.

Slapstick

Slapstick is fast and zany physical horseplay for comic effect, such as a seemingly drunken man falling down an open manhole. The most familiar example, though, is a cream pie thrown in someone's face. There are certainly hostile elements here, but no one gets hurt (hopefully), and children and many adults find such rowdy interactions funny. This accounts for the ongoing popularity of Charlie Chaplin, Buster Keaton, and the Three Stooges.

Surprise

Surprise is the occurrence of an unexpected outcome that can then become the punch line. For example, Sam innocently asks his brother, "Have you seen Mom around?" "No," his brother replies, and then gets punched in the nose because Sam no longer fears being discovered by Mom. Of course, the element of surprise is also the key to the fun in infant peek-a-boo games. (See "The Peek-a-Boo Game" on page 33.)

Verbal Humor

Verbal humor is specific humor resulting from the manipulation of language, as in riddles, word play, puns, jokes, sarcasm, wit, and name-calling. Of all the forms of verbal humor, jokes, puns, and riddles are the forms most favored by kids. As such, they deserve some special attention here.

Jokes

A joke is a very short story that has been stripped of all non-essential details to create a humorous effect. For example, for younger kids: *"If you want to catch a squirrel, climb a tree and act like a nut."* And, for older kids: *"Two cannibals are eating a comedian. One asks the other, 'Does this taste funny to you?'"* Of course, there are all different types of jokes, including knock-knock jokes. *"Knock-knock. Who's there? Goliath. Goliath who? Goliath down, you looketh tired."*

Puns

A pun is the use of a word that can have a double meaning or the use of two similar-sounding words for a humorous effect. For example, the word "blue" can refer to a color or a mood; "flies" can be insect pests or the action of a bird or airplane; to their children, parents can appear to be "all-knowing" or "all no-ing." A high school music teacher penned a clever pun when he posted this sign on the door of his office: "Out to lunch. Bach at 1 p.m. Offenbach sooner."

Riddles

A riddle is a misleading or puzzling question posed as a problem. Although some riddles can be merely word games or puzzles without humor, the answer to a riddle is often intended to be clever or funny: *"How do you keep a fish from smelling? Cut off its nose!"* A variation of this form is the *punning riddle* (also known as a *conundrum*) in which the answer to the riddle is a pun. *"When is a horse not a horse? When it turns into a barn."* Or *"What kind of music do you listen to in the car? Cartoons."*

The answer to a riddle is often too difficult for a listener to discover on her own. When the teller reveals the answer, the listener will then learn how the incongruity posed in the question can be resolved. Children must have sufficient cognitive development to "appreciate" that resolution and enjoy the riddle. The riddle poser by definition feels "superior" to the listeners because the listeners do not know the answer to the riddle—and rarely can figure it out if the riddle is new to them.

It's usually easy to appreciate a joke when it presents an unresolved incongruity, but in riddle form any unresolved incongruity can create a kind of cognitive tension that is inconsistent with humor making. The listener often feels foolish for not being clever enough to figure out the solution, which seems "obvious" when heard. Riddles, like puns, seem to create more pleasure for the teller than for the listener and rarely produce hearty laughter, but this fact doesn't (and shouldn't) stop kids from telling them.

Violence

Violent humor is the release of hostility through aggressive actions. For example, cartoon characters may throw one another off cliffs or conk one another over the head with a skillet. Most adults do not see these examples as funny. The popular Three Stooges films contain lots of violence—sticking fingers in others' eyes and hitting others over the head with hard objects. (Understandably, their movies are enjoyed more by boys than girls.) Children should be reminded that such actions are *not* real and should not be imitated—especially during their ritual of watching Saturday morning cartoons.

STAGES OF HUMOR PREFERENCES AND DEVELOPMENT

In general, the type of humor that children prefer as a group follows a regular developmental pattern. Individual children, however, will naturally differ in how long it takes them to reach a certain stage. Just as kids vary in their height or social skills, they vary in their humor skills. So, it can be a bit misleading to say, for example, that five-year-olds think this particular riddle is funny but eight-year-olds do not. Sometimes a given comment, joke, or pratfall will be funny to most children and even to most adults. Knock-knock jokes are the stock and trade of five-year-old comedians, but haven't we all heard some adults tell and genuinely laugh at a knock-knock joke? Despite the great variability in this puzzling field of humor, we can make some general remarks about what is funny at certain ages and why it is funny. Remember, these age guidelines are very rough.

Babies and Toddlers

Laughter is baby's "simple pleasure." Laughter results when parents smile at their babies, make silly faces, tickle them gently, and so on. The well-known peek-a-boo game is one of the first instances when a baby's humor emerges. *Surprise,* the violation of expectations, is the crux of the peek-a-boo game and the major form of humor in babies and toddlers. (See "The Peek-a-Boo Game" on page 33.) Since language development is, at its best, very primitive during this time, only physical stimuli—for example, gentle tickling, sudden noises and movements, and lifting the child up in the air—may elicit laughter.

Soon to follow in the child's development of humor will be some appreciation of essentially visual humor in the form of slapstick. For instance, the child might laugh at someone harmlessly hitting someone else with a pillow or wearing a big red plastic nose or purple wig.

As language comprehension begins to develop, the toddler will be on the road to responding to verbal humor, particularly in forms such as nonsense and silliness. Rhyming and nonsense names will be funny because of their *sounds,* not the meanings of the words. Even making non-word noises will be regarded as funny to these very young children, perhaps because of the inappropriateness of not saying real words.

Once a familiar pattern develops in the child's thinking, and she becomes better able to detect the more subtle incongruities in her environment, the potential for humor is created whenever an expected pattern is disrupted. For example, a talking banana is funny to a child who knows that bananas do not talk in real life (except to other bananas). An adult sitting in a sandbox, wearing a diaper, and sucking on a bottle will seem funny to a child who is aware that adults do not ordinarily act that way. Missing objects in scenes will seem funny to a child who is confident about what should be present.

Preschoolers

A preschooler's perception of something is more important to her than her intuition or thinking. This means that the way something looks rules her judgments, even if she "knows" otherwise. For example, if you have a glass of water and you pour all of that water into a larger glass in front of the child, it will not rise as high in the second glass. The child has seen that you have not taken any water away. Yet, the child will conclude through visual perception that there is now *less* water in the second glass.

How does this relate to humor? It means that perception, rather than logical thinking, will influence what is funny to the preschooler. When knowledge conflicts with appearance, the latter will dominate at this age. These children will laugh at a picture of a bicycle with square wheels, but will not be able to appreciate the logical incongruities of riddles, puns, and jokes. However, their language may humorously show *conceptual incongruities*. At this age, children are aware of the various characteristics of a given concept such as a particular animal. For example, if you call a picture of a dog a "horse," it will be funny. If you say the dog goes *moo*, it will sound funny. The source of humor for them is the incongruity of the sounds or pictures with what they know to be true of that concept or object.

Gender differences are especially prominent issues for a child this age. So, if someone refers to a boy by a traditional girl's name, such as Sue or Cheryl, children at this stage will note the inconsistency and laugh. The humor would be lost if a genderless name, such as Sandy or Chris, were used. Clearly, the child's language abilities must be sufficiently advanced to appreciate this kind of humorous incongruity.

Child development specialist Beverly Allred Schroeder notes that a playful frame of mind is more likely to appear in pre-schoolers during vigorous physical activities than during intellectual and fine-motor tasks, when the child is more likely to be serious and concentrating on details. Schroeder concludes, "Pre-school humorists, those youngsters who make others laugh, are likely to be energetic and aggressive both verbally and physically. The critical factor in developing a sense of humor seems to be a lot of opportunities for social play. An audience and an ever-changing play situation stimulate verbal inventiveness and physical clowning. Other children's responses play a central role in building up the habit of being funny and laughing at others' humor. Preschool children also seem to be funny purely for the fun of it."

Children Ages Five to Seven

The jokes and riddles told and enjoyed by this age group are not likely to require formal logical thought processes. This child's thinking is quite subjective and very concrete. Humor is more likely to come from physical gestures and play. Slapstick humor is highly appreciated, along with socially unacceptable topics like bathroom humor. Subjects that most people find strange or sad are particularly enjoyed at this age: *"I saw a dirty man pushing a shopping cart full of empty cans"* (laughing loudly). Exaggeration to the point of ridiculousness is a typical form of humor: *"I'd like a million zillion pieces of pizza."* Even some elementary forms of word play may appear now, with familiar words in simple riddles or variations of proper names: *"My new teacher is Mr. Jones-Bones."*

Children of this age typically have discovered that joke-telling gets them lots of attention. They also thoroughly enjoy the social power that comes from being able to make others laugh. There is a sense of "I know something that you don't" felt by the joke teller, who knows the punch line. Children of this age also are familiar with the rhythm of conversations, and their joke-telling comes more easily. Kids do not hesitate to repeat jokes time and time again, even to the same listeners. It's fun to be funny!

Children Ages Eight to Ten

In this group, there is more variety seen in the preferred types of humor: puns, more complicated riddles, stock jokes, and laughter at any deviation from conventional behavior and dress. Taboo topics, such as bodily functions and sexually related body parts, are not taboo to eight- to ten-year-olds. The physical humor of slapstick eventually gives way to more subtle, verbally based humor in the middle childhood years. A child in this age group will demonstrate a more spontaneous wit and be able to detect comical aspects in the irrationalities of daily life: *"Why do hotdogs come in packages of twelve when hotdog buns come in packages of eight?"*

Kids at this stage seem to be preoccupied with riddles or stock jokes—like moron or knock-knock jokes—and will repeat them endlessly. They may have the same topics of interest as five-year-olds, but in more intensified and refined ways. These children are now able to perceive and create sympathetic humor and can channel negative feelings into positive humorous situations.

Children Ages Eleven to Twelve

At this stage, children not only repeat jokes and riddles they've heard, but also create new humorous comments as potentially funny situations present themselves. They tend to enjoy verbal and witty humor over the visual and physical humor preferred by younger children. Their increased skills in logical thinking are now reflected in their humor preferences. Thus, jokes and riddles become more sophisticated and more influenced by biologically based drives.

When children reach this stage, the aggressive and sexual content of their humor tends to increase. Ultimately, they become skilled at using humor to achieve their own specific social goals. As a child begins to establish a clear and independent self-image, her humor preferences reflect that concern and the newly felt importance of interpersonal relationships. The difference between sexes becomes more pronounced at this stage: boys initiate humor more, and girls laugh more but initiate less.

Children Ages Thirteen and Up

The humor preferences of children in this age group are very adultlike. More complex jokes are told, and their themes and language may be very explicit (and often offensive to parents and other adults). The humor of irony, reality-based incongruity, and socially awkward situations are now common themes. Individual differences in children's senses of humor are well established. Many kids at this age have developed the capacity to laugh at themselves, as well as insulting and ridiculing their peers and parents. However, if you follow the guidelines presented in this book, by the time your child reaches this stage, she should have a healthy sense of humor—even if she thinks your jokes are awful.

HUMOR IN CHILDREN'S LITERATURE, TELEVISION, AND MOVIES

There are many types of humor found in children's literature, on television, and in movies. Usually, humor books that are written specifically for children are not questionable regarding the appropriateness of their content. Television and movies are, of course, another story. What is intended to be funny and get laughs isn't always appropriate for children.

A very important part of developing your child's sense of humor is providing a humor-rich environment for your child, which includes generous exposure to humor in children's literature, television programs, and feature movies. To be sure, though, passively reading or watching humor will not be enough to increase your child's sense of humor. It's important that in addition to these activities, your child also participate in humor-related social activities.

Literature

According to Michael Cart, expert critic and reviewer of American humor books for children, these books consist of three main types: 1) talking animals—a universal form of fantasy humor; 2) tall tales—stories about larger-than-life heroes or stories that convey absurdly incredible falsehoods; and 3) family comedy stories. To that, let's add joke and riddle books and comic books with humorous characters like Archie and Jughead and the Peanuts gang.

Whatever form the humor takes in children's literature— satirical comments on our culture, slapstick comedy, nonsense rhymes, unpredictable silly behavior, and so on—you can rest assured that your child will benefit greatly by having these books read to her or by reading such books on her own—or even to you! It's great fun to read humorous books aloud.

Television

Parents are not as likely to watch television with their children as they are to read with them. It's far too easy to allow children to watch television with minimal supervision or involvement. For this reason, many parents may not be aware of the types of humor presented on children's television.

The Peek-a-Boo Game

One of the first instances of children's humor emerges with the well-known peek-a-boo game. The peek-a-boo game is fun for babies because there is a momentary threat—Mom or Dad has disappeared (the threat) but quickly reappears (the surprise). This works best with babies who feel relatively secure.

At this early level of cognitive development, babies assume that if they cannot clearly see something, it must be gone or it does not even exist anymore. Peek-a-boo involves major shifts in emotion and perception. To the infant, Mom's or Dad's face goes from existence to nonexistence and then back to existence. Babies who feel personally secure are able to retain confidence that Mom or Dad is not gone permanently. And, sure enough, that is the case. Baby then expresses delight by smiling and laughing at the surprise. (For details, see page 69.)

Adults enjoy the peek-a-boo game as much or more than babies do because they are being handsomely rewarded by seeing their infant smile and laugh. The serious adult player might want to read Sheila Hanly's book *Peek-A-Boo! 101 Ways to Make a Baby Smile*.

The peek-a-boo game can provide double degrees of fun later on, when baby learns to initiate the game by hiding her own face and then showing it to her parents. Everyone laughs and shares in the fun, and baby is definitely well on the way to developing a great sense of humor.

Non-cartoon television programs designed for young children typically use humor as a vehicle to support their main goals of teaching about the world—how to get along with others, the behavior of animals, and elementary facts such as the alphabet and the names of colors. These shows, however, are not comedy shows. Bert and Ernie from *Sesame Street* are a pair of funny guys, but they are not comedians. Interestingly, the Public Broadcasting Service (PBS) series *Zoboomafoo,* which emphasizes learning about animals in enjoyable and safe ways, concludes each program by telling jokes and riddles. The humor contributes to the show's goal of making learning fun.

Cartoons on television are often more violent than they are humorous. It is more accurate to refer to them as animated programs rather than as funny shows. The vivid colors, rapid actions, and lively music all are attention grabbers for young children. As children get older, they become more aware of the story lines and the occasionally deliberate inclusion of double meanings of words. Still, the message cartoons often send is that hurting others gets laughs. In all fairness, some children's cartoons are genuinely humorous and harmless. Watch a few cartoons and see which ones you approve of.

In the *Encyclopedia of 20th-Century American Humor,* Alleen and Don Nilsen summarized the role of humor in children's television programs: "Contemporary programs for toddlers and preschoolers are filled with light-hearted music, happy or silly characters, soothing voices, familiar settings and situations, and theme songs promoting the feeling that every child is loved and the world is a happy place. In such shows as *Barney, Teletubbies, Mr. Rogers' Neighborhood,* and *Sesame Street,* the humor is mostly based on surprise, exaggeration, and incongruity. Children giggle at the surprise of a small, stuffed dinosaur changing into the big goofy Barney, while on *Sesame Street,* they laugh at the exaggerated size of Big Bird and the incongruity of a Muppet prancing with a professional ballet dancer."

Thus, there is plenty of humor in young children's television programming, but it is there primarily to enhance the delivery of other messages. When children reach school age, other programs such as *Arthur, Between the Lions, Dragon Tales,* and family-oriented situation comedies become more appealing. The themes of these shows often involve trouble at school, coping with an absent parent, or other social changes that are eased by the use of humor. Humor appears throughout the programs, but it is not the main purpose. There are also adolescent variety shows, in which young comedians do silly sketches. The humor in these shows is geared toward adolescents and teens, but younger children may also find the shows humorous. Be forewarned, though; the humor in these programs often pokes fun at adults.

Some networks—Nickelodeon, for instance—shows "old" situation comedies that were originally broadcast when today's parents were children themselves. These shows are less likely to be offensive than today's sitcoms because in those bygone days, writers vigorously avoided "sensitive" social topics.

Older children become increasingly adultlike in their television comedy tastes. Their interests in relationships, drug use, and yes, sexual matters, are booming. These topics, of course, are rich lodes for professional comedians to mine. Children's television is a tremendous medium for children's learning. What they learn, though, is often controversial. So, be sure to watch television with your child every chance you get.

Movies

Many movies can entertain children while helping them develop a healthy sense of humor. In some cases, movies are specifically designed as comedies—although they may also convey messages about values and relationships. In the case of many movies for small children, though, humor is used to support a dramatic story line, but is not the main purpose of the film.

How can you know whether a given feature film is appropriate for your child without attending it yourself—and perhaps having to leave in the middle and ask for a refund? Take advantage of the comments of professional movie reviewers on television, in magazines, and in newspapers. You usually can learn if a movie is indeed funny (from a child's perspective) and if there are any objectionable aspects to the movie. Some local newspapers even have reviews of movies *for* kids written *by* kids. They can be quite helpful to concerned parents.

By all means, go to the movies to see comedies and rent funny videos with your child, but make sure the movies your child sees are age appropriate. (For more information, see "Movie Theaters" and "Video and DVD Rental Stores" on pages 151 and 155, respectively.)

CONCLUSION

You have seen how children move through recognized stages as their sense of humor emerges. As with any ability, these skills develop at different rates. Children will prefer certain types of humor in roughly the same order, but it is impossible to restrict these preferences to certain ages. Some forms of humor that children enjoy remain popular for their entire lives. We all know some adults who regularly watch cartoons, even when no kids are present.

With your new awareness of the different categories of humor that children enjoy and the stages of humor development, you are now better equipped to nurture your child's sense of humor. But first, let's look at the roles of play, smiles, and laughter in your child's life.

CHAPTER 3

Play, Smiles, and Laughter

Shared laughter is love made audible.

—IZZY GESELL, HUMORIST

HAVE YOU EVER WATCHED a small child build something out of blocks? Is he playing? Sure. Is he smiling? If he's pleased with his accomplishment, perhaps he is. Is he laughing? Probably not—not until he knocks the blocks down and sees your surprised reaction. This is just a small example of playing, smiling, and laughing all occurring during one activity. Clearly, they are three different things, but people tend to see them as parts of the same process. Therefore, in this chapter, we will discuss the roles of play, smiles, and laughter not only as they relate to your child's sense of humor, but also as separate concepts. Separating these related terms should help you understand their functions and how they can reflect changes in humor expression in your child. This chapter will also describe the wonderful physical benefits of laughter and even provide tips on increasing the laughter in your child's life.

PLAY

Play is a term that adults use to describe behavior that is supposed to be fun—as opposed to that negative term "work." However, in the very youngest of children, play really takes the form of exploratory behavior as children manipulate objects such as toys, and learn about their environment. These children are not actually demonstrating or experiencing humor. Any pleasure they feel comes from their mastery of the object, solving the problem of moving it from here to there, or simply picking it up to look at it closely. Sometimes this playlike behavior is referred to as *nonsocial play* or *solitary play*. Although this form of play declines with age, it's still the most frequent style seen in three- to four-year-olds.

Around twelve months of age, children for the first time exhibit *parallel play*, which includes a social component. In parallel play, they continue to play by themselves but in the presence of other children. At the same time, they display a keen interest in what the other children are doing. Each child plays separately and may respond if the others move, speak, or squeal. Adults do this, too: one watches TV while the other reads the paper. They are presumably enjoying their respective activities and are aware of the other's presence, but they do not really interact during these times. Parallel play remains frequent and stable throughout the preschool years from ages three to six.

Between one and two years of age, the more social forms of play emerge. In *associative play*, children continue to pursue separate activities but do show some coordinated interaction by exchanging toys (sharing) or by commenting on one another's behavior. A more advanced form of social relationship emerges as *cooperative play*, in which the children's behaviors are oriented toward a common goal, such as acting out a story together, building a tower of blocks or Lego bricks, or holding and feeding a doll.

Play is simply what young children *do.* It is not particularly a way for them to have *fun,* as we understand it, or to experience humor. What is important about the various types of play is the accompanying development of social skills and language abilities, both of which will be helpful in increasing the children's appreciation and use of humor.

So, when kids play, are they demonstrating their sense of humor? Strictly defined, the answer is "no." Kids may indeed be having fun and enjoying their games, whether the games are fantasy play (like pretending to be a mermaid or an astronaut) or structured play (like the card game Go Fish, board games, or even Little League baseball). Pretending to be something you're not is fun for kids (adults, too) because they are not constrained by the usual social rules that apply to them as themselves. And what's fun about structured play is the excitement of a challenge, of interacting with others, and of competition. Solving a puzzle can bring great satisfaction, and the spirited rivalry of trying to win a game can be very pleasing and thrilling. Yet, these fun experiences are something different from children demonstrating their sense of humor.

Eventually, though, play behavior does become associated with fun and with humor. Humor is sometimes defined as "intellectual play" because it involves intentionally perceiving or creating different ways of using words or objects for the purpose of having fun. Most animals—monkeys, dogs, cats, and parrots, for instance—play with humans or other animals. But animals cannot verbalize their perceptions and attitudes about what they are doing. If they do something funny during that playtime, they don't know that what they are doing is comical. They may recognize the pleasure that their behavior elicits, but will not consciously think, "Hey, I'm one funny animal!" A true sense of humor requires the kind of cognitive abilities that only humans possess. We have the capacity to observe ourselves during play—and at all times—and to develop perspectives on those observations, some of which are funny. And that is when a sense of humor emerges in play.

SMILING

Smiling and laughter are actually quite different reactions. They can occur together, or smiling can appear alone without overt laughter. Adults are capable of feeling amused without revealing it through smiling or laughing—but not children. Children are less defensive than adults. They do not hide their emotional reactions to events, positive or negative. If they are unhappy, they will cry. If they are happy, they will smile.

Many things make us smile, and they certainly don't have to be humor related. Freshly baked chocolate chip cookies with milk, a rainbow, a gift, a kind gesture—all of these things and more are apt to produce a smile in almost anyone, young and old alike. And, of course, a good joke is always sure to produce a smile.

Although sometimes you can't help but smile, smiling also can be a voluntary act produced at will. In fact, a smile is not always "genuine," although it typically has positive effects on other people. A salesman or con artist (not always the same person) can use smiling to improve your attitude toward him and induce you to part with some of your money. In other situations, a smile is a deliberate friendly greeting that will most likely be well received and returned by the recipient—and possibly result in a social relationship. A smile also serves as a play signal to others, indicating that what you're about to say is intended to be humorous or kind. This pattern works for both children and adults. (See "Play Signals" on page 81.) However, smiles in a newborn are another thing entirely. "Oh, he's just passing gas," you might hear someone say in response to a newborn's early smiles. So, when do a newborn's smiles become "genuine"? When do babies begin to smile and laugh in response to humor stimuli? For these answers, see "Smiles and Laughter in Babies" on page 42.

LAUGHTER

We're all familiar with the sound of genuine laughter—the body's physical response to the perception of humor. When something's funny, we laugh (or chuckle, chortle, giggle, titter, guffaw, and so on). With so many words for laughter of different degrees, it's a wonder we don't do it more often. Of course, laughter can also occur without humor—with physical stimulation and in stressful situations. Laughter can also be faked and manipulative (especially by adults). This artificial behavior should not be encouraged in children, although sometimes it's okay to be polite and chuckle at a friend's failed attempt at humor, as long as the joke was not offensive. Taunting or derisive laughter, which is a hostile act toward someone who has made a mistake, is not humor based and should not to be encouraged. These aren't the laughs we're after. You are set on a course to help your child learn to use humor to evoke genuine laughter in others and, of course, in himself.

It seems obvious that laughter improves relationships, but did you know that laughter also helps our bodies function more efficiently and healthfully? Below, we'll discuss these health benefits of laughter, and in case you're not entirely clear on what is *not* considered laughter, we'll take a brief look at that. Then, we'll wind up with a discussion on how to increase laughter in your child.

Smiles and Laughter in Babies

Smiling and laughter occur for quite some time before children actually experience humor. Overt laughter is not seen in the newborn. However, two forms of smiling are ordinarily observed: endogenous smiling and exogenous smiling.

Endogenous smiling, sometimes called "false smiling," arises from within the newborn because of internal stimulation. It occurs from birth onward during rapid-eye-movement sleep. Thus, it looks like a smile to us, but, in fact, it is just a physical phenomenon having nothing to do with any type of humor source. Endogenous smiling decreases in the first few months and disappears completely by six months of age.

Exogenous smiling occurs in response to some kind of external stimuli and develops in the first two months after birth. These are indeed real smiles but are not true social smiles. The best stimulus for these early smiles is a soothing voice, and after five to six weeks, a human face may elicit this response. Most developmental psychologists agree that the critical time for predicting when a baby will smile is not the infant's actual age, but the baby's *conceptual age.* Conceptual age is a function of the baby's degree of neurological and cognitive development. All babies smile once they reach a conceptual age of forty-six weeks.

Smiling is a newborn's second most common way of communicating, and the parents' most preferred. Crying to indicate a desire for feeding or changing works very well for babies. No one really *enjoys* hearing them cry, and every effort is made to get them to stop and be content again. But a smiling baby is something else entirely. The baby's look of obvious pleasure is heartwarming.

Within a couple of months, babies begin to smile at Mom and Dad, whose faces and voices have become familiar. Soon, beginning at around three months or so, babies are able to laugh out loud spontaneously. The thrill is unmatchable, and parents go to great lengths to repeat the experience. Parents play with their babies by making funny faces, imitating the baby's gestures and sounds, cooing, playing peek-a-boo, and talking baby talk, all in an effort to coax laughter from their little ones.

At around six months of age, babies begin to laugh at interesting things, such as the smiling sun on the *Teletubbies* program, and at incongruous events, like when Dad puts a banana on his head. By the end of the first year, infants are capable of displaying sustained joy and elation. In the second year, toddlers smile and laugh in actual anticipation of funny things happening. At this point, the child is neurologically capable of forming mental images of events and of developing humor as part of fantasy play.

Remember Charles Gruner's humor theory discussed in Chapter 1—that humor is based on the notion of winning or losing? This is what he has to say about smiles and laughter in infants: "Infants do not smile or laugh when *not getting what they want*. Indeed, smiling and laughing always occur when the baby is experiencing pleasure; that is, when he or she *is* getting what he/she wants." The baby, then, is winning, and if that's what a baby's smiles and laughter are all about, parents are sure to let their babies win every time!

The Biological Benefits of Laughter

Genuine laughter is one of the most beautiful sounds in the world. Not only does it make your child feel good to laugh, but it also makes you feel good to hear it. As TV journalist Diane Sawyer notes, "The laughter of kids is great for the immune system of parents!" But it doesn't stop there. The child who is laughing derives many wonderful health benefits. Unlike so many other pleasures, laughter *is* actually good for you.

Hearty humorous laughter benefits the body in many ways. For example, the act of laughing can help us endure pain more easily. Some physicians suggest that the effects of *endorphins*— morphinelike chemicals that create "natural highs"—released from the pituitary gland in the brain during laughter can raise our pain threshold. These good feelings are drug-free and tax-free.

Dr. Margaret Stuber, a psychiatrist at the University of California at Los Angeles, recently demonstrated the physical benefits of laughter to children. Using a standard laboratory stressor— the ice immersion test—the doctor asked healthy kids to hold their hands in ice water for as long as they could stand it. Those kids who, at the same time, were shown funny videos—Abbott and Costello, the Marx Brothers, and Lucille Ball—were able to leave their hands immersed for an average of 40 percent longer than those who did not watch the films. (One interesting sidelight to Dr. Stuber's research is that the antics of these classic comedians, recorded several decades ago, were found to remain funny to kids of today.) Dr. Stuber's research showed quicker recovery from the stress of the ice immersion and improved blood pressure, heart rate, and immune functioning because of the kids' exposure to humor.

Healthful laughter—genuine laughter in response to appropriate humor stimuli—involves a number of body systems: respiratory, muscular, circulatory, and gastrointestinal. During laughter, our respiratory and cardiovascular systems get a work-out—breathing becomes more rapid and blood pressure is temporarily elevated. Muscles tighten as well. As the physical laughter subsides, the positive benefits become clearer: breathing slows, deepens, and becomes more regular; and heart rate, pulse, and blood pressure return to below their resting levels at least for a short while (until the next good laugh); the muscles return to their relaxed condition, partly resulting in better digestive functioning. Dr. Herbert Lefcourt, a researcher at the University of Waterloo in Canada, put it more succinctly. After studying the ability of a humorous perspective on life to moderate the effects of external stress, Dr. Lefcourt described people with a good sense of humor as "physiologically serene."

In addition, other studies have documented improvements in immune function after exposure to humor. Interestingly, in many of these studies, researchers actually measure an antibody released in the salivary glands, which is already known to be associated with better immune responses to stressors or invading bacteria and viruses. When patients open their mouths in laughter, medical researchers take swabs of their saliva to demonstrate that laughing results in clear physical health benefits as well as "mere" pleasure.

Much of this biological research is in its early stages, but thus far, there are *no* studies reported that have found negative physical effects from genuine laughter. Perhaps hearty laughter could result in pain for patients with a broken rib or those healing after recent surgery. Even then, the pain is mixed with pleasure. Medical literature describes some rare clinical cases of inappropriate laughter due to brain tumors or severe psychosis, but even in these patients, their laughing, per se, was not harmful to them. Many of us have "died laughing," but no one has died *because* of laughing. Thus, we can safely conclude that when your child is laughing, he is receiving biological benefits to his body. I, of course, recommend that those physical gains be supplemented with the more traditional forms of exercise and physical play.

Theodore Geisel, better known as Dr. Seuss, taught us that laughing is the best thing that kids do of all the things they do. Kids will laugh—spontaneously and uncontrollably—until their sides hurt. It is their "pain of having fun." When was the last time you laughed so long and hard that you felt "side stitches" or tears actually fell from your eyes? When was the last time your *child* actually fell down laughing?

Laughter Not Associated With Humor

Children laugh long before they are able to talk or understand language. For example, adults love to tickle children to see and hear them laugh. This laughter is technically not a product of humor because the child is responding to a sudden physical stimulation to the underarms, ribs, neck, backs of knees, or feet. Frequently, tickled children laugh a lot, but do not enjoy being tickled. In the worst cases, tickling is abusive and hostile. I advocate tickling only on an occasional basis, and always as part of a broader positive emotional interaction with children.

Similarly, tossing a child into the air might produce smiles and laughter in the child. Again, this is not humor. The child is responding to the sudden and fear-arousing kinesthetic sensations of being high in the air without support for those few seconds. When the baby is quickly caught by the adult (which, by the way, we *always* recommend!), the child is reassured, feels safe again, and may smile and giggle.

We should note that some people smile and laugh when they are socially anxious or even fearful in the presence of actual danger. Obviously, such laughter is also not indicative of humor and is indeed not especially adaptive behavior unless it dissuades an enemy from attacking!

Increasing Laughter in Your Child

Psychologist Robert Provine of the University of Maryland has studied laughter in all of its manifestations for over a decade, trying to understand the often hidden laws of laughter. Although writing for adults, he offered a number of laughter tips for bringing more laughter into our lives. We can readily adapt some of his recommendations to encourage more laughter and humor appreciation in our kids.

☐ *Realize that it only takes a minimum of two people to produce laughter.* To produce social laughter, a child and one parent or friend are sufficient. Stuffed toys and live pets aren't much help in reaching that social minimum. Humor attempts and games between two people almost always result in shared laughter and fun. You can set up these conditions by using humor yourself with your child and by arranging for another child to be available to interact with your child. Instead of arranging play dates for your kids, you can arrange "humor dates," and laughter will

surely follow. Laughter is often described as "contagious"—it becomes easier to laugh when you are with one or more people who are also laughing. Good humor, like a juicy secret, is best enjoyed when shared with someone.

☐ *Recognize that the more people there are sharing the humor experience, the more laughter will result.* Dr. Provine refers to this phenomenon as the "social multiplier effect." At a live comedy show or in a movie theater, a large crowd laughs more than a small crowd. So, instead of inviting just one child over, invite several kids over to play humor-filled games. Also, take your child to public places that offer humorous entertainment, like comedy movies specifically for kids.

☐ *Be ready to laugh!* Create a casual and laughter-prone environment for your child. The best way to do this is to model a readiness to laugh yourself. Keep a low threshold for your laughing response and your child will learn to do the same.

☐ *Be aware that frequent laughter requires a lowering of social inhibitions.* Luckily, children are much less inhibited than adults.

The Laughing Parent

In the Southwest of the United States, a Native American tribe gives special status to a new baby's "laughing parent." The laughing parent, who is not necessarily the child's biological parent, is the adult who can first produce a laugh from the baby without actually touching him. A special relationship is thus created with the laughing parent and lasts for the child's lifetime. This custom is certainly worth adopting in all cultures.

That freedom should be encouraged as often as possible, within the limits of considering the feelings and rights of others, and the appropriateness of the situation.

☐ *Design family activities around just having fun together.* Sharing jokes, arranging birthday and holiday parties, and watching a video together (prescreened by parents for its humor content) are all great laughter-producing activities.

☐ *Provide lots of potential humor stimuli for your child.* Funny pictures, joke and riddle books, videos of comedy movies, toys such as "Tickle Me Elmo," fun games, and so on can all help to serve this purpose.

Many things will make kids laugh. We can and should encourage them all. You'll find Chapters 5 and 9 very helpful in this respect.

WHAT HAPPENED TO THE CLOWNS?

Humor is not just joke telling or riddle posing. Humor really comes from adopting a certain, perhaps tilted, perspective on the world. That perspective will change over time, just as what a child thinks is funny will change over time, as he develops cognitively and emotionally. The fun of identifying and laughing at the absurdities and illogic in our world, though, should not change. Laughing at the humorous creations of others, such as jokes or movies or stories, should not change. Finding humor in our own mistakes, blunders, and limitations should not change. Smiling and laughing *with* others should not change. Unfortunately, when we reach adulthood, to some degree, all that does change.

On average, young children laugh at least 200 times a day. Dr. Madan Kataria, founder of the international Laughter Clubs movement in India, claims that children actually laugh 300 to 400 times each day! Adults on average, though, laugh only 15 to 18 times a day. Who stole those 285 or so laughs a day from us as we "matured"? When did our parents and substitute parents—teachers, activity group leaders, clergy, coaches, and others—train us not to laugh so much? Who dictated that mature, sober, responsible, adults should not laugh frequently at work, at school, or while playing sports? What an outrageous disservice to us and to our society. As the song says, "Send in the clowns!" and let's all keep laughing!

CONCLUSION

After reading this chapter, you should have a better understanding of play, smiles, and laughter. Clearly, they are not always part of the same experience, although they quite often occur together. You've also learned about the many wonderful benefits that laughter can have on the body. And you've learned some ways to increase laughter in your child. But don't stop here. There's so much more to come.

CHAPTER 4

Developing Your Child's Humor Skills

*They (children) learn to laugh, as they learn to talk
and walk, and are most apt to laugh profusely,
when they see others laugh. . . .*

—DAVID HARTLEY, PHILOSOPHER

HAVE YOU EVER NOTICED THAT some people seem to have no sense of humor whatsoever? If something is serious, they quickly comprehend. If it's funny, they just don't get it. For them, humor plays an insignificant role in their lives. It is likely that very little went on during their formative years to cultivate an appreciation of humor. Could something have been done long ago to broaden their view of the world? Absolutely. Although it may be too late for them, it's certainly not too late for your child. In this chapter, you'll discover that there are a number of specific steps you can take to help your child develop her humor skills so that she will grow up to be an adult who laughs. Helping your child develop her sense of humor won't always be an easy task, but it will be an ongoing fun-filled way of spending time together.

THE THREEFOLD STRATEGY FOR DEVELOPING HUMOR APPRECIATION

Can a simple strategy help you develop your child's appreciation of humor? Well, having a strategy can make it easier, but that doesn't necessarily mean it will be easy. It will require your understanding of the issues involved and a commitment to make humor an everyday occurrence in your family's life—both inside and outside the home. The threefold strategy—modeling humor-related behavior, shaping humor with humor support, and removing social barriers—is introduced below, and its individual elements are covered throughout the chapter.

1. *Model the specific humor-related behaviors you want to encourage in your child.* Modeling is a technique in which a person consciously exhibits specific behavior in the hope that it will be imitated. Since your child has plenty of opportunity to observe the things you say and do, the most powerful humor-teaching technique is the simple creation or enjoyment of humor in your child's presence. This can be demonstrated both in positive settings, where fun and humor are anticipated, and in potentially negative situations—for instance, when a drink has been spilled. The key is to not only set aside specific times to engage in humor and humorous activities, but to *model* your own lighthearted attitude and readiness to smile or laugh at the funny side of everyday occurrences.

2. *Shape humor in your child with humor support.* Shaping is a general technique that involves rewarding all attempts at the desired behavior no matter how crude they may be, and then becoming more discriminating with those rewards until the desired level of behavior is reached. For example, with a very young child, you can begin by supporting all efforts at humor

with praise, no matter how unfunny the efforts are, and then gradually become more demanding by raising the standard little by little over time. Humor support can be a few words of praise or can involve a variety of positive reactions, such as laughing and "playing along" with the joke or contributing additional humor.

3. *Remove the barriers to humor appreciation that society typically erects for kids.* Too many of us retain the antiquated notion that adults should always be serious and that children should not share their thoughts and opinions, humorous or otherwise, with adults. Children should be taught that being adultlike doesn't mean life has to be taken seriously all the time or that the joy of humor should be reserved for only special occasions. Kids should be encouraged to speak up spontaneously in most situations and share their funny observations and comments, even in the company of adults.

THE EFFECTS OF FAMILY, FRIENDS, THE MEDIA, AND SOCIETY ON HUMOR APPRECIATION

An appreciation of humor is acquired largely through demonstration and observation. Kids learn what is funny and when it is okay to express their amusement through laughter from four main sources: their parents, other kids, the media, and society. Keep in mind, however, that although your child may be learning to appreciate humor from sources other than your family, you may not always approve of *what* she is learning to appreciate. It's a good idea to encourage your child to talk openly about jokes she hears on the playground or sees on television and in movies, and then to discuss your feelings—both positive and negative—about her experiences.

Parents

Children learn about life by observing the other people in their lives, especially Mom and Dad. They learn to appreciate humor by being part of a family that appreciates humor and freely demonstrates their appreciation for what is funny with smiles and laughter. Through interactions with you, your child can learn that humor is appreciated and that you want her to contribute to the family fun by laughing and sharing all forms of humor. When everyone in the family shares jokes and riddles, laughs during funny scenes on television, and tells humorous anecdotes from their daily lives, children will quickly catch on to the value of humor.

Older Siblings and Other Kids

What kids learn from other kids about humor is largely out of the direct control of the adults in their life. As with many other kinds of information and values, peers and older siblings represent very strong influences on children. Older brothers and sisters are especially powerful role models for young children. They affect attitudes and behaviors of all types, including how to define what is funny and how to be funny. Once a child begins to attend school, learning from friends tends to increase, while learning from parents and older family members tends to decrease.

Children teach one another that some forms of humor—jokes about sex or bathroom functions, for instance—are best not shared with adults. Keep in mind that the types of humor that children bring to the playground are usually a result of their early humor experiences at home, which we hope were positive but may not always have been. Once again, be sure to talk with your child about the humorous comments her friends and classmates may make. Hopefully, you'll just get a good laugh out of

your talk, but if not, refer to Chapter 6 for a discussion of abusive humor and how to deal with it.

The Media

Children also learn what is intended to be funny by watching television (canned laughter often tells them what actions or words they *should* think are funny), by going to the theater and observing the reactions of those around them, and by being read to by people who affirm humorous points through their own laughter. Even children who read on their own—a magazine with a joke column, for instance—learn to recognize what is intended to be funny, and probably develop an appreciation for such humor.

Society

Rather than learning *how* to appreciate humor from society, as they grow, children are often taught how *not* to express or appreciate humor. This can explain why so many children who are naturally full of joy eventually grow up to become "jocularly challenged" adults—that is, people who have difficulty laughing or recognizing the humor in the world.

In our culture and in most cultures, adulthood is a status given to people who can be described in terms such as reserved, mature, serious, sober, businesslike, professional, deliberate, controlled, concerned, grave, and so on. The wealth of dour terms used to describe adulthood reveals just how serious this problem is in our society. All of these somber qualities—without an equal balance of lighthearted qualities—are distinct inhibitions to a joyful, humor-filled life. These restrictive qualities are often taught and enforced by the accepted agents of society—parents, teachers, group leaders, childcare workers, and others.

Certainly, over the years, many teachers, coaches, and strict parents have clearly informed kids that there shall be "no laughing," "no joking," and "no smiling" in class, on the field, or at the dinner table. Nowadays this guideline is really appropriate only in very serious situations—when attending a funeral, visiting a hospital, or witnessing an accident, for instance. The good news is that in most other settings in American society, that old value of humorlessness *is* changing. As a progressive nation, we are recognizing more and more the value of humor as a stress reducer, as a health promoter, as a pleasing personality trait, as an aid to learning, and even as a facilitator of corporate productivity and comfortable working relationships. Consultants are increasingly offering humor-building seminars to hospital patients, to educators, and to business people to improve both their personal and professional lives. Perhaps if more of us take the time to help our children develop their sense of humor, these remedial seminars for adults will someday become unnecessary.

While we've come a long way in removing the social barriers to humor appreciation, there's still more work ahead. There are a lot of people out there who were raised to believe that humor is inappropriate, especially on the part of children, in most situations. When we *all* agree that businessmen, doctors, lawyers, teachers, police officers, accountants, and other professionals can possess and display a sense of humor, even at work, we will have made some much-needed progress.

PROMOTING ASSERTIVENESS

A major step on the journey to enhancing your child's sense of humor is the promotion of certain qualities that will create a positive-humor environment. These characteristics include personal assertiveness, a quality that allows an individual to express herself in a bold, self-confident manner; and empathy, a sensitivity to the feelings, thoughts, and experiences of others. Assertiveness is discussed below, while empathy is covered in Chapter 6.

To be assertive is to share, to speak up, to contribute to a conversation, and to express one's real feelings, all in the context of courtesy and social appropriateness. The concepts of children's humor-making and assertiveness skills actually are very closely related. For a child to create humor and then to share it with others is clearly an assertive act. The humorous and assertive child is one who readily appreciates the humor in the world, who can create humor by inventing funny responses or humorous observations, and who is willing to share her humor with peers and adults.

To be humorous and assertive is somewhat of a social risk for anyone—but especially for a child. Some adults might verbally chastise a child who contributes something funny to a conversation for being a "smart ass" or "wise guy." Even when the assertive comment is not humor related—if a child dares to speak up and offer a different point of view—some adults may silence her with phrases like, "Don't you speak unless spoken to" or "It will be that way because I say so!" I still remember seeing a calendar on my grandmother's kitchen wall with boldly printed parenting advice in the form of this maxim: *Children should be seen and not heard.* Luckily, my wise grandmother did not follow this ridiculous recommendation, but I clearly remember feeling rather uneasy and unhappy upon reading it. Unfortunately, many authoritarian parents and adults do strictly follow these kinds of inhibiting childrearing values. Their children will be the least likely to develop strong senses of humor.

It's important to teach your child that her humor efforts are welcome and will not be frowned upon, and that her opinions and thoughts will be valued. Assertive children feel comfortable about speaking up and expressing their feelings, desires, and humorous observations. Most of us appreciate those behaviors in adults and should by all means encourage them in children.

MODELING HUMOR

Modeling—consciously acting in a specific way in the hope you will be imitated—is a scientifically well-documented method of teaching new behaviors. It is especially useful for teaching complex behaviors. Indeed, the ability to appreciate and create humor requires complex skills. To fully develop a sense of humor in your child, you can use this process to freely demonstrate your appreciation and use of humor in front of her whenever the opportunity arises—which, ideally, will be quite often.

How do you go about doing this? With toddlers, you can read humorous comics or Dr. Seuss books aloud. You and your spouse can joke with each other or report humorous events that happened that day at work in front of your child. You can laugh aloud while reading something funny in the daily paper or in a book, and share what made you laugh with those present. Your family can watch a television show together, such as those seen on Nickelodeon or the Disney Channel, or spend a family night at the movies seeing a comedy and laughing out loud at the funny parts.

Other opportunities to model humor and the appreciation of humor will occur spontaneously. It's important to remember that the development of humor appreciation in kids is not a one-time effort. You can't just schedule it for some special Friday night and accomplish your goal. It must be ongoing, and it must occur in a humor-enriched home and humor-nurturing family environment. There will be countless opportunities every day to note, share, and model humor. Casual observations of funny things at work, at school, or in the community can be shared at dinnertime—or at any time your family gets together.

When everything is rosy and pleasant, it's relatively easy to demonstrate the enjoyment of humor in the family. However, "negative" events in which no one gets hurt can be a challenging time to model humor. Consider a situation in which someone spills a glass of milk at the dinner table. This happens occasionally in *every* family (trust me on this one). A possible response to such an event is that of anger and critical comments directed at the perpetrator, but it doesn't have to be that way.

Let's say that one of the adults, Mom or Dad for instance, spilled the milk. Most likely he or she would not be chastised for the accident. So why yell at and punish a child for making the same mistake? After all, no one *wants* to spill milk, and no one will become malnourished due to the loss of one glass. It was an accident, and no one has gotten hurt. Of course, the spiller should clean up the mess—if she is capable of it—but why not accompany the whole incident with some humorous comments? The spiller will feel less guilty, and Mom and Dad will feel less angry or maybe not even become angry.

What can possibly be said that will be perceived as funny in the midst of this great "tragedy"? You could make a comment that takes off on the old cliché "There's no use crying over spilled milk," by quickly saying something like, "All right, nobody cry!" (For a remark like this to be funny, everybody at the table needs to be familiar with the old cliché.) If an adult is the milk-spiller, another adult can jokingly say, "Just for that you have to go to your room without dessert." (Adults are rarely serious about such a comment.) Or, if it is a child who spilled the milk, as is most often the case, you can lightheartedly say something like, "Don't worry. The cows can make more!" or "I didn't know you liked milk with your green beans!"

These examples are not intended to illustrate hilarious humor (luckily). Our main point is that modeling some humor at a potentially stressful time such as this, even humor of a relatively poor quality, will ease the emotional strain on everyone present. Things could be a lot worse. Rough spots in the road will always be a little easier to navigate when humor is added as a shock absorber. Modeling humor during negative events will prepare your child to use humor as a way to counteract the stresses of everyday life.

The process of modeling is most effective when the model is successful—that is, when what the model does or says is genuinely funny—and when the observer is rewarded for mimicking the model. The observer, the child in this instance, can be rewarded with humor support as part of the shaping technique. This concept is discussed in the following section.

SHAPING HUMOR WITH HUMOR SUPPORT

Shaping, a technique discovered by behavioral research psychologists, can be effectively used to establish a new behavior. The shaping procedure involves rewarding successive approximations of the ultimately desired target behavior—that is, rewarding increasingly closer examples of what you are trying to teach. Usually, explicit praise that is delivered enthusiastically in the context of laughter and smiling is the most effective way to reward and shape the new humor-making behaviors. *"That's very funny!" "What a riot!"* In this way you are supporting your child's humor efforts with *humor support,* and your child then knows immediately that what has been said or done has been received as funny and is pleasing to the parents. That attention and praise (and love) are the strongest possible rewards to a child for developing any new desired behaviors at any age level.

If you model your appreciation of humor as described in the previous section, your child will soon try to be funny by doing or saying things in special ways. A young child's early attempts will probably be shaky and not very humorous. However, this will be your opportunity to begin using the technique of shaping by rewarding these early attempts, no matter how crude, with humor support.

It is crucial to be generous with your approval and to praise your child's early humor efforts. For example, when your preverbal child does something intended to be funny, you can quickly and joyfully laugh and exclaim, "That's funny!" The child will realize that her efforts were noted and approved, and will feel emotionally warm and accepted. The phrase "That is funny," when it is accompanied by your own laughter, an approving tone, and maybe even clapping, will be very rewarding to your child, which will result in her making attempts at humor again and again.

What can a preverbal child do that she might think is funny? Well, as babies and toddlers begin testing out their voices, they may make sounds (or even screech) to win the attention and approval of their parents. When those sounds are accompanied by smiling, the child is expressing her sense of humor. For this, parents can laugh and praise the child. But as the child grows, this isn't a behavior a parent would want to continue to encourage, so parents should become more discriminating in rewarding the child's humor attempts. A more refined display of humor than just a laughing scream would be a child setting a toy on her head or hiding her face behind a cap. Because these objects are obviously not intended for that purpose, the effect is funny. You can laugh along, and verbalize what is funny and why: *"A toy truck is a funny hat. That is funny." "You fooled me by hiding behind your cap. That is funny."*

It's important to recognize that shaping is a general strategy. It can be used, however, to shape interest in particular forms of humor—such as riddles or jokes. But shaping should be used to encourage all types of appropriate, inoffensive humor.

We talked about providing humor support in the form of laughter and the phrase "that is funny." But humor support can be more involved, especially for older children. *Humor support* is a concept from the field of communications research that can be specifically used by parents to help develop their children's sense of humor. It refers to your response to someone who tries to say or do something funny. If those humor efforts are rewarded by laughter and obvious enjoyment by others, they will soon be repeated. Behavior that is rewarded will tend to recur. This effect is one of the strongest laws existing in behavioral psychology.

Jennifer Hay of Northwestern University describes four possible components of humor support that can occur in the response of the audience—recognition, understanding, judgment, and agreement. In the case of humor, the audience can be as small as one other person in social contact with the child. That person, often the parent, can *recognize* and acknowledge that what was said or done by the child was an attempt at humor. In that way, the parent can communicate that the humor was *understood* and possibly *judged* as funny. A parent's smile and/or laughter suggests that the parent *agrees* with the humor message and the accompanying assumptions that underlie it.

If the humor attempt is off-color, racist, or sexist, it could very well be funny, but you may not agree with such attitudes and may not want to encourage those attitudes in children. In that case, you may choose to withdraw humor support entirely and explain why the attempted humor was not acceptable. Alternatively, you can laugh at a comment, thereby communicating your appreciation of it as truly humorous, but then quickly follow up with your reasons for disagreeing with the message. For example, you can quickly add, "That's cruel" or "That was in poor taste." However, the opposite is not possible: you cannot laugh and then deny that you appreciated the humor. By laughing, you indicate that you did appreciate it. Thus, you can verbally cancel your agreement with the underlying, perhaps offensive, message of a joke, but you cannot cancel your agreement that it was funny. In these instances, you want to clearly explain to your child why such material is unacceptable (more on that in Chapter 6). This is all part of shaping appropriate humor in your child.

Humor support is critical for the development of humor efforts by adults, as well as by children. To make a joke and then get no response or a negative response is like offering your hand for a handshake and getting no takers. You usually learn quite quickly not to repeat that mistake, whether it is a poor joke, a joke in poor taste, or both. Kids learn quickly, too. We want to help them distinguish between appropriate and inappropriate types of humor without discouraging them from trying out their budding humor wings. So, be generous with your humor support, but use it wisely to shape your child's sense of humor into a characteristic that can be enjoyed by all.

CONCLUSION

In this chapter, we have reviewed the most important techniques and strategies for increasing your child's humor skills. The strategies include providing a humor-rich environment, encouraging rather than punishing assertiveness, modeling humor, and shaping humor with humor support. These are sure-fire keys to success in developing your child's sense of humor.

The concepts of positive reinforcement and constructive feedback are well established in any training program. We know that rewarding a behavior will increase the chances that it will occur again. Similarly, ignoring or correcting a behavior with negative feedback will decrease the chances that it will occur again. Your laughter, praise, and expressions of joy and approval will be highly rewarding to your child and will result in your child's making attempts at humor again and again. The humor will gradually become sharper and clearer. Over time, it will also become more subtle and sophisticated.

The next chapter examines several activities that will promote humor creation in your child. For best results, remember to use the strategies you learned in this chapter while you and your child are enjoying the activities in the next one.

CHAPTER 5

Encouraging Your Child to Create Humor

It is so important that families take time out to play together.
Experiencing laughter, fun, and adventure creates memories
that will be brought up year after year with a smile.

—SHEILA ELLISON AND BARBARA ANN BARNETT,
AUTHORS OF PARENTING BOOKS

MICHAEL CART, AUTHOR AND LITERARY CRITIC, points out, "Laughter is like a piano; it needs to be practiced." In fact, *both* humor and laughter have to be practiced. Comedian and musician Steve Allen reminded us that learning how to be funny is much more complex than learning how to make music. It may be more complicated, but practicing laughter is certainly a lot more fun than practicing the piano! This chapter offers a number of ways in which you can develop your child's humor-creation abilities, including creating and recognizing everyday humor, choosing what's right for your particular child, using specific age-related humor-creation exercises, and employing play signals—"warnings" that what's about to follow is intended to be funny.

EVERYDAY HUMOR

You can make humor part of almost any daily activity you engage in with your child. Feeding your infant or bathing your baby can be a fun, humor-filled activity, although each has another primary purpose. For example, moving a spoonful of food through the air while making the sound of an airplane can make the chore of eating more enjoyable for most kids. In the bath, pouring warm water like a waterfall over your baby's head can be more fun than scary if you laugh gently and make a game of it. Learning to catch a ball can be a frustrating task for many young children, but that process can also be made more fun by using humor. For example, for every successful catch your child makes, you must make up a riddle or put on a big red clown nose, or something equally silly. For older children, you can keep a special joke book to offer as a treat when certain everyday chores are accomplished. For example, if your child cleared the dinner dishes from the table (or took out the trash or swept the front walk), he would have access to this joke book and be allowed to pick out a joke to tell to the entire family. This special joke book would not otherwise be available to your child.

Grandma's Rule is a standard technique that grandmothers have been using "naturally" (meaning without any scientific research support) for many years. In somewhat more technical terms, Grandma's Rule involves making a reward contingent upon the occurrence of specific desirable behavior. For example, a child would be rewarded with an ice cream dessert only if he ate all his vegetables. How can Grandma's Rule be applied to humor creation? Once the child completes his homework (or studies for an hour or finishes ten math problems or whatever), he can watch a half-hour comedy show on TV or play the "Create a Caption" game described on page 75 of this chapter.

Dinnertime is an especially good opportunity to incorporate humor into your everyday routines with your child. Having a family meal together each evening is a valuable tradition for many reasons beyond humor enrichment. In many modern families, this practice gets lost because of extra work demands on parents and the typical "hyper-scheduling" of children's after-school activities. A shared meal should occur at least once a day, and dinner is the best time for Funny Family Time! At this meal, Mom, Dad, and each child in the family can take a turn telling a funny story about what happened that day. If a funny incident does not come to mind immediately, a standard joke or riddle can be substituted. The first choice, though, should be a real-life event because that will encourage everyone to adopt a humorous perspective throughout the day.

Beginning on page 68, I will discuss specific activities that you can arrange with your child to help him create humor, but my strongest general recommendation is that you try to incorporate humor in as many of your child's *everyday* activities as possible. Your child will soon learn that almost anything can be partly fun (even homework).

WHAT'S RIGHT FOR YOUR CHILD?

Before we get into the specific suggestions of humor-creation exercises that you can share with your child, it's important to keep in mind that the exercises you choose must be consistent with your child's stage of development—verbally, emotionally, and intellectually. Therefore, you should regard the suggested age guidelines as fairly rough because of the vast differences in individual children. Don't worry if your child doesn't seem to respond much to a particular exercise for his age group. He will probably have a more positive response soon. In the meantime, simply choose another exercise. Nobody follows strict charts of progress, whether it's for height, weight, or the age of taking a first step or becoming potty trained. For example, certain forms of verbal humor, as explained earlier, require that a child understand the meaning of key words, which may indeed have several meanings. If the humor creation involves props, such as wigs, magic markers, or juggling, the child must first possess the motor skills to manipulate the materials. It is better to be very conservative in what you ask your child to do.

Creating humor will be a fun task, but because it is a new skill, your child may be very tentative at first. It is much better not to frustrate your child by asking for behavior that is a little too difficult in terms of existing skills. Rather, ask for things that you know are already well within your child's comfort zone. Similarly, your child must be comfortable in the "performing" role—if the exercise involves any kind of performance. Even telling a riddle at the dinner table or making a funny face on command is a kind of performance. Overly shy children can do it, of course, but you will want to move just a bit more slowly with them and accompany their "training" with lots of modeling and encouragement.

HUMOR-CREATION EXERCISES

The suggested exercises in this section should be done *with* your child, not assigned as independent homework. You should be present to deliver praise and provide feedback on the child's "work." These suggestions are only representative and certainly not meant to be exhaustive. They should serve to stimulate some ideas of your own, or modifications and extensions of the present exercises, as you try them.

Some psychologists who conduct research on the development of cognitive abilities in children claim that kids cannot show true humor until around the age of two. However, the exact age at which your child can actually create humor is less important than your building a genuine *appreciation* of funny things in your child and setting the stage for your child's actual humor making. Thus, the following material suggests specific humor-related exercises geared for kids of different ages, from newborns to twelve-year-olds. Why are we leaving out the teenagers? Well, as mentioned previously, once a child enters the teenage years, the degree of influence from parents declines markedly. However, if you do have kids in their teens, it won't hurt to encourage them to participate in some of the activities along with you and your younger child, as long as they show a willingness to model appropriate humor and genuine enjoyment of the chosen activities.

EXERCISES FOR NEWBORNS TO AGE 1

Funny Faces

Attempt to get your child to laugh at things you do and say, such as making funny faces or quickly rocking your head back and forth so that your hair flies around (this is not to be tried by balding fathers!). At first, your child's laughter will be a response to this humor stimuli, but in time your child will be laughing and imitating the laughter-producing behaviors, which better illustrates humor creation.

The Peek-a-Boo Game

Play the peek-a-boo game (see page 33 in Chapter 2). In the first stage of this game, hide your face behind a screen such as a blanket and then quickly take the screen away. The goal of this stage is to get your child to smile and laugh. Technically, it does not involve humor *creation* by your child; however, in the second stage, when your child can initiate the game by hiding his own face and then pulling away the screen, this really *is* humor creation! Similarly, children may hide their eyes, assuming that you can't see them because they can't see you. It becomes great fun to have them peek out to surprise you by revealing that they were there all along.

Physical Stimulation

It is possible to produce smiling and laughter in babies through various forms of physical stimuli: gentle tickling or holding your child high and suddenly bringing him down without letting go. The informal theory here is that getting the baby to smile and laugh, even by physical means, helps establish neural pathways for those behaviors, which can later be invoked in response to more intellectual or cognitively based humor stimuli. At the very least, the process of *mild* physical stimulation in a fun and laugh-filled context can be an emotionally enriching experience for both you and your child.

Silly Sounds

Make silly sounds or imitate your child's unique noises while smiling and laughing. Smiling and laughing defines your behavior as funny, and soon your child will be clearly displaying his enjoyment of your antics. The specific sounds you make will vary with different children. It could be a forced panting or even whistling through your teeth, which has never failed to gain the attention and smiles of my son Sam since the age of three months. Sammy didn't seem to understand where the sound was coming from or how it was made, but he always laughed.

Sing Songs

Sing a well-known children's song like "Pop Goes the Weasel." Once your child is familiar with the song, you can make a dramatic pause before adding, "POP!—goes the weasel!" The child will anticipate the pause, feel the comedic tension, and then laugh loudly with the punch line "Pop." Of course there are many different songs to which you can add your own comedic effects. When your child begins to sing them on his own, you may notice—to your delight—that he adds his own humorous twists to the lyrics.

EXERCISES FOR AGES 1 TO 3

Add-Ons

Sing any well-known nursery rhyme and add the phrase "in the tub" to the end of every line. The incongruity and surprise is what is funny to the child who is expecting to hear the very familiar lines of the jingle. For example, Rock-a-bye baby—*in the tub!* In the treetops—no, *in the tub!* When the wind blows—*in the tub!* And so on.

Crazy Animal Sounds

Pretend that certain animals make the sounds of other animals, for example, the cat goes "bow wow" and the horse goes "cock-a-doodle-do." (This exercise is funny to kids once they know what the correct sounds are that are associated with the various animals. Before then, there is no humor, but there may be confusion.) Take turns with your child choosing an animal and then demonstrating a sound that *doesn't* go with that animal. See how long a series you and your child can create by repeating the pre-

vious ones on the list. Do animal number one; then one and two; then one, two, and three; then one, two, three, and four; and so on. For example, at number one, the rooster goes "baa baa"; at number two, the doggie goes "moo moo"; at number three, the kitten goes "bow wow"; and so on. Do not fear that this game will permanently confuse your child. The fun comes from the difference between the associations that the child has previously learned and those created in the game. Besides, in real life, does a dog *really* say "bow wow"? Does a rooster really say "cock-a-doodle-do"? Not on my farm!

Rhyming Names

Make up funny rhyming names for friends, relatives, or pets—for example, "Silly Billy" or "Clumsy Mumsie" or "Bitty Kitty." The rhyming sounds are probably the key to their funniness for these very young children because there is no logical sense to the humor. Kids this age will tend to laugh heartily. Eventually, they'll try this verbal silliness on their own.

EXERCISES FOR AGES 3 TO 6

Acting Out

Pick words or pictures out of a hat, and then act them out, or have your child act them out, for others to guess. When your child gets a little older, he will be ready for the parlor game of charades using children's movie and book titles and everyday phrases. Such games will promote your child's socialization skills as well as his talent for humor creation.

Mimic Animal Behavior

Suggest that your child pretend to be a pet animal and act as such an animal would—for example, serve a bowl of dry cereal on the floor and suggest that your child eat it with no hands. Obviously this exercise is one to do only on certain occasions. It will be funny partly because it mimics the behavior of a family pet, but largely because this is a type of behavior that on most days parents would not encourage.

Rhymes

Play the silly rhymes game: choose a word—any word—and follow it with rhyming nonsense words or real words. For example, busy, dizzy, tizzy, fizzy, and so on. As children start to master language and the meanings of words, this game allows them to show off their accomplishments by using words in silly ways without meaning or logic. (If they become really skilled at this game, they could have a bright future in the world of greeting cards.)

Staring Contest

Have a staring contest with your child. Whoever laughs first "loses" the game and then must do something funny or tell a joke or ask a riddle. At first, this may sound like an anti-humor technique, but it actually turns into great fun for kids in this age range.

Strange Colors

Put a few drops of food coloring in familiar foods to change them into unfamiliar colors—for example, make green mashed potatoes or blue milk. Let your child choose the color. The different colors will be funny to kids who have already learned to expect the normal colors in those foods, but have not yet learned to associate these colors with spoilage.

Did you know that catsup is now available in different colors? Try surprising your child with green or purple catsup next time you serve French fries.

EXERCISES FOR AGES 6 TO 9

Backward Dinner

Plan a "backward" dinner with your child for the following evening's dinner—the first course would be dessert, followed by side dishes, the main course, and finally soup or salad. Have your child pick the courses that will be served and the order in which they will be served—for example, ice cream, pie, or cookies? Mashed potatoes, stuffing, or noodles? Broccoli, peas, or carrots? Chicken, fish, or steak? and so on. Your child can even help prepare the meal.

Create a Caption

Get a group of children together to read the Sunday comics, and set aside several strips that are only moderately funny. Then have a brainstorming session during which everyone tries to make up different or funnier captions for the cartoons. *Brainstorming* is a problem-solving procedure used by groups to increase creativity by generating many possible responses to a question without evaluating their merits until all the responses have been made. After the captions have been created, you can all evaluate them for their humor potential. Brainstorming is a useful technique here because it allows for a variety of possible creative responses.

Of course, if there are only two of you, you can still do this exercise—there just won't be as many captions to evaluate.

Funny Stories

Make up a funny story with your child with extreme exaggerations of the events and people's characteristics. You can start the

story and pause to have your child fill in exaggerated descriptions. For example, you can begin by saying, "This is an untrue story about Tall Tommy. Tall Tommy was so tall that when he walked down the street, his head touched the _____."
At this point, your child could say, "street lights" or "clouds," or whatever might sound funny. Then you would add, "Every time tall Tommy's head hit the <u>clouds</u>, it would start to rain. The rain was so heavy that _____," and so on. It might be necessary for you to give some examples before asking your child to participate, or you may need to help your child think up some funny exaggerations.

Funny Uses

Think of funny uses for common objects, such as bananas, combs, or tennis balls. The exercise of thinking up uncommon uses for familiar items draws upon your child's creative abilities and basic intelligence. When you add the goal of devising unfamiliar uses that are *funny*, the exercise becomes an ideal tool for humor development. For example, you could use a banana as a paperweight—in addition to its usual use as food, of course. That, however, would not be funny. A funny use of a banana would be to employ it to measure the distance from the television set to your favorite chair. You may even add, "Eye doctors have warned us that you must sit at least thirty banana lengths from the television."

Ha, Ha!

Play the "Ha Ha" game. This one works with any number of participants. The first person says, "ha," the second one says, "ha ha," the third person says, "ha ha ha," and the game keeps going around the room until everyone is laughing too hard to continue.

Riddles

Talk about why certain riddles are funny. Consider this riddle: *"What did one eye say to the other eye? Just between you and me, something smells."* This riddle is funny to kids six to nine years old because it deals with body parts and double meanings. You can use other funny riddles and discuss just why they are funny. Once some general points about riddles are understood, it will be fun for your child to make up some brand-new ones with your guidance.

Word Play

Similar to the "Funny Stories" activity, you and your child can invent funny exaggerations as part of imaginative word play in single sentences. The creations should be unrealistic and physically impossible in order to increase their funniness. For example:

It was so hot today that the trees melted like ice cream in the sun.

I wish I were so strong that _____.

The test was so hard that _____.

The first cookie I ever baked _____.

The movie was so funny that _____.

I laughed so hard that I _____.

EXERCISES FOR AGES 9 TO 12

Cartoons and Captions

Draw cartoons with your child and make up captions for them. This game takes the "Create a Caption" exercise one step further by asking your child to actually use his imagination to create the drawing before coming up with a humorous caption for it. Even rough line drawings will work here because the main idea is to produce creative humor, not polished artwork.

Comedy Show

Help your child put on a comedy show for family and friends. This activity could also involve some younger children, but the older ones are needed for structure and organization skills. This is a fairly high-level task for the demonstration of humor-creation skills. It could be considered the "final exam" of your humor-development program.

Greeting Card Humor

Read some humorous greeting cards together, and then try to make up a punch line that is even funnier than the one printed in the card. This exercise can be done on the spur of the moment in a card store, while actually searching for a card to buy for someone. Ordinarily, the so-called "humorous" greeting cards tend to be only moderately funny at best, so this exercise can be a real confidence booster to a child whose own verse may well be funnier than the printed version. This exercise makes the point that humor-creation exercises need not be preplanned in great detail and that potential humor stimuli are all around us.

Halloween in July

One day in July—or on any summer day—dress up in Halloween costumes along with your child and go around to friends' houses and knock on their doors. When they answer, say, "Trick or Treat!" Halloween is always a fun day for kids. To do it twice a year is at least twice the fun, and to be able to enjoy the startled reactions from surprised friends only adds to this fun.

Out-of-Season Holiday Songs

Sing Christmas carols or other out-of-season holiday songs around the barbecue grill on the Fourth of July. The incongruity and the inappropriate timing can make this a fun activity for children who are old enough to recognize these elements and who know the words to the songs. It will give the holiday a special meaning beyond that of parades, ballgames, and hot dogs.

Puns

Talk about what puns are (for a reminder, see page 25 of Chapter 2) and whether all puns are funny. Discuss why puns usually cause the listeners to groan rather than laugh heartily. Try to make up some *funny* puns as a joint exercise with your child. I assure you, it will be great "pun and games."

Reverse Order

Wear your clothes in reverse order with your undershirt on the outside, new boxer shorts over your slacks, and socks over your shoes, and then go about your day normally. You can model the behavior if you want, or you can suggest it and encourage it in your child. To enjoy this game, your child must have some well-developed social assertiveness. This behavior will surely provoke some interesting and humorous comments. This exercise can be done at home, in the neighborhood, and in parks, but it is not recommended for school (where "they" will say it "disrupts the learning environment").

Tongue Twisters

Try to rapidly verbalize some standard tongue twisters, and then make up some new ones together. For example, start with short ones like "black bugs' blood" or "the sun shines on shop signs," then move on to longer twistable sentences such as, "Betty beat a bit of butter to make a better batter." Older children will enjoy creating their own sentences, and will especially enjoy the verbal errors that result from rapid repetitions.

What Happens Next?

While watching a comedy video with your child and his friends, stop the tape at key points and have everyone guess what will happen next. (Be sure no one has already seen this particular show or movie.) Considering the possibilities will stimulate everyone's comedic imagination. After various ideas have been suggested, play the tape to see what happens next. Right or wrong, the results will be enjoyable.

The Humor Center

Establish a Humor Center somewhere at home, where any family member can post funny cartoons they have seen, jokes they enjoy, witty quotes, or descriptions of funny and amusingly embarrassing things that have happened. The Humor Center could be a bulletin board in the family room or even the front of the refrigerator, although it may already be filled with your child's drawings, pictures, notes, and so on. Be sure that whatever you use, there's plenty of room so that everything added to it can be easily viewed.

The concept of the Humor Center brings home the concrete reality that humor is encouraged and appreciated in your family. Humor is to be enjoyed and shared by one and all. The center will serve to stimulate everyone to be alert to possible humorous items and topics in the everyday world that can be documented and shared with other family members.

What's Funny About Not-So-Funny Things?

Discuss what can be funny in situations or topics not ordinarily thought of as humor arousing: for example, sitting in math class, watching baseball games, or observing a trial on Court TV. In these situations, humor will arise spontaneously and unpredictably. For example, San Diego Padre Rickey Henderson hit a record-breaking home run over the wall, rounded the bases, and came sliding into home plate.

Court TV televises actual criminal trials of real defendants and genuinely serious events, but it can be humorous to catch a glimpse of the judge nodding off or the defendant drawing cartoons on his yellow "legal" pad. And in math class, catching the math teacher's simple arithmetic error can be a funny event (to the students, if not the teacher).

EXERCISES FOR EVERYONE—AGES 3 TO 12

Funny Home Videos

Make home videos of your child trying to say and do funny things. He will surely laugh during the taping—even when what he is doing is not very funny by anyone else's standards—and will laugh harder when viewing the videos immediately afterward and at future times over the years.

Humor Props

Obtain some humor props for your child—for example, a plastic nose, oversized shoes, huge bowtie, bubble-blowing kit, balloons, cowbells, and the like. Wearing and using these items are clear "play signals" that humor is being communicated and laughter is expected. (See the discussion of play signals on page 82.) Since many clowns do not talk (unless under a court order), verbal skills are minimized in this activity.

Make Me Laugh

Play the "Make Me Laugh" game. This can be done with several children simultaneously. Each child gets one minute to make Mom, Dad, or another adult laugh by telling a joke, making a funny face, doing a crazy dance, or whatever. The time available can be varied, but the exercise works best with a period of one to two minutes. The game requires both spontaneity and creativity, and has a built-in audience (other kids and adults) for social rewards. Using a kitchen timer can heighten the tension and fun for older kids, but should be omitted with younger kids to minimize pressure.

Monkey See, Monkey Do

Take a trip to the zoo and watch the monkeys. Imitate their behavior as it's happening, right next to their enclosure. This exercise requires some assertiveness and lack of social inhibitions in your child. You can begin the fun by imitating the monkey models first. Monkeys are our not-so-distant relatives, yet they are not as emotionally sensitive and do not seem to mind being mocked by laughing children and playful adults.

PLAY SIGNALS

When your child plans to make a humorous comment or gesture, it is often very helpful if he first gives a "play signal"—some sign that indicates your child's humorous intentions. Why are play signals so important? They help ensure that there is not a miscommunication between the child and his audience. (In this case, the term "audience" can mean just one other person or many people.) Play signals are especially important when your child is attempting humor with adults in authority, such as a teacher or sports coach. If he makes it clear that an upcoming message is meant to be humorous, the adult is less likely to take the comment the wrong way. Younger children require a greater amount of and more obvious play signals from others than do older children. Even when adults interact with one another, they need to use play signals, such as a phrase like "Did you hear the one about . . . ?", which informs the listener that what follows is intended to be humorous.

A play signal can be just a subtle smile that tells the audience that what is about to be said is not really intended to be serious. In other cases, your child can mention that he has heard a new joke or riddle and can ask if you would like to hear it. Also, play signals can be very obvious, with or without an accompanying smile: Using props, such as an oversized plastic bat or a giant colorful umbrella with gaping holes in it, leaves very little room for doubt that what's to follow is intended to be funny or is *already* funny. Sometimes a physical setting can be a play signal itself—an amusement park or a birthday party, for example. In those settings, joking, crazy costumes, and other fun surprises are expected.

Be sure to use play signals around your child so that he can learn from your example. You can even create your own play signals to be used occasionally—a ringing bell, a funny face, clapping twice, or whatever. The possibilities are unlimited.

CONCLUSION

In this chapter, I presented a number of suggestions for humor-creation exercises for you, your child, and other children to enjoy. I have organized the activities according to rough age guidelines with the understanding that because of individual differences in skill and comfort levels, you will have to choose the particular activities that best suit your child. If an activity is a little difficult for your child, save it and return to it in a few months. In the meantime, one of the other exercises may prove to be a big hit. Some of the exercises require more verbal skills than others. Some work better when other kids and adults are also involved. Be sure to use your imagination to come up with your own ideas, too, while keeping safety, comfort, and appropriateness in mind.

It is essential that you take part in these exercises to supervise, reward, and ensure that inappropriate humor and language are not being used. The next chapter will discuss possible ways in which humor can be abused so that you can be on the lookout for such problems. However, when engaging in the activities mentioned in this chapter, try to be part of the fun, not merely an observer.

CHAPTER 6

Potential Abuses of Humor by Children

Sadistic humor is deriving humor from witnessing the physical or psychological harm of a person . . . Inappropriate humor is taboo in its subject matter or target . . . (and) includes sexist humor, racist humor, and sexual or bodily function humor.

—AMY M. BIPPUS, HUMOR RESEARCHER

AS YOU'VE LEARNED BY NOW, HUMOR is a powerful tool and technique, but it *can* be used inappropriately and abusively. Any force or substance powerful enough to do good can also cause harm when misused—be it a new wonder drug on the market or the newly acquired skill of humor. We must, therefore, give serious attention to the possibility of the misuse of humor skills by children.

Children are often unaware of the devastating effects abusive humor can have on the intended targets, on themselves, and on society in general, and often have difficulty figuring out exactly what humor abuse is. Adults and children alike need to know the limits of humor, when to modify it, and when to restrain it entirely. Successful humor training includes teaching your child when not to use humor and which types of humor are inappropriate for kids.

What children learn in their early years will carry over into adulthood; you can make sure that your child understands the differences between what is funny and what is cruel so that she can put her humor skills to good use throughout her life.

WHEN KIDS SHOULD NOT ATTEMPT HUMOR

Throughout the process of encouraging humor appreciation and creation in your child, you should discuss appropriate times and places for using humor. We certainly don't want to fall into the old-fashioned idea that laughter should be restricted to certain situations, but admittedly there are some times when children should *not* attempt humor out of consideration for others. Such situations might include visiting someone in the hospital who is seriously ill, attending a funeral or religious service, or being present at a serious accident or crime scene. Professional comedians and some adults might attempt humor in these situations, and as long as they are sufficiently skilled and sensitive to the feelings of the people affected, that's usually okay. But no matter how seemingly funny, it is best for most people *not* to attempt humor in serious situations.

At a later time, you and your child may find some of the happenings at these events humorous, but they should be shared *at that later time.* One of the standard formulas for comedy is "tragedy plus time," which means that *anything* can become a topic of humor once sufficient time has passed to allow for emotional distancing. Deaths of loved ones, war, and even disasters may be treated with humor after some time. George Bernard Shaw once wrote, "Life does not cease to be funny when people die any more than it ceases to be serious when people laugh."

HURTFUL HUMOR VERSUS HEALTHY HUMOR

Children are not as capable as adults of distinguishing between hurtful humor and healthy humor. We all undoubtedly know some adults with the same difficulty, but our focus here is on helping children avoid humor that can be unfair or abusive. As beginners, children need to be taught very explicitly how to distinguish funny comments and actions from those that will have negative effects. It's very important for them to understand the features of humor that are hurtful and the features of humor that are helpful. Hurtful humor is disruptive to personal relationships, while helpful humor improves relationships as well as increases a child's sense of worth and well-being. For example, the comment "You're as fat as a hippo on a holiday" might get a laugh, but it is very hurtful to an overweight individual. Teaching children how to define healthy humor and how to avoid hurtful humor often allows us to provide important moral and human value lessons at the same time.

Humor that is safe and appropriate for children has either the child herself or society's institutions as its targets; humor that is hurtful and inappropriate involves specific individuals or groups as its targets—ethnic or religious groups, the physically or mentally unhealthy, or socially unfortunate or marginalized people, for example. There are obviously many jokes in which specific groups are viable targets for humor. Satirists and professional comedians operate in this realm almost exclusively, but for children, I recommend the complete avoidance of humor that might be hurtful—psychologically or physically.

Children should not make fun of their friends, families, or other adults in their lives when the presumably humorous point is the target's skin color, religion, ethnicity, health, appearance, fashion tastes, speech, sexual orientation, or unique personal values and beliefs. Such topics *might* be acceptable for humor in some adult situations, but even then this sensitive territory is difficult to navigate successfully. In the table on page 89, I've summarized the characteristics of appropriate and inappropriate humor for children, with an example of each.

INAPPROPRIATE HUMOR

In the spirit of knowing thine enemy, we must discuss several of the most common types of inappropriate humor—that is, regardless of the topic or the target of the humor, we can think of instances in which that particular humor might be considered unacceptable. For example, the essence of Don Rickles's comedy act is hostile put-down humor. His audiences expect it and enjoy it. Our interest here, though, is humor that is inappropriate for children, and that is a much longer list than humor that is inappropriate for adults. In general, we do not recommend any kind of humor for kids or by adults that is explicitly sexual, excessively hostile, or ethnically or religiously insensitive.

Hostile Humor

Although humor is a normally delightful ability, it can unfortunately be used specifically as a weapon to ridicule, humiliate, and degrade its targets. Humor has had a longstanding close relationship with aggression, which is revealed by some of the phrases in our language that refer to the use of humor—for example, we use terms such as "killed," "ribbed," "mocked," "cut up," "roasted," "knocked them dead," and many others to describe the effects humor has on the audience or target.

Unfortunately, having a well-developed sense of humor means that a person may enjoy hostile humor as well as the more positive types of humor. Generally, this book tries to promote the

Appropriate Humor	Inappropriate Humor
Self-directed	**Other-directed**
"I'm pretty funny—funny looking."	*"Even my dog is smarter than you."*
Applies to all people	**Applies to specific group**
"Why is it we can pick our friends and we can pick our noses, but we can't pick our friends' noses?"	*"Did you hear about the blond who shot an arrow into the air and missed?"*
Decreases tension	**Increases tension**
"Why was 6 afraid of 7? Because 7-8-9!"	*"He's so skinny that if you put a flag on his head he could be a flagpole."*
Promotes hope	**Predicts hopelessness**
"If the rain keeps up, it won't come down."	*"Wife finds her husband at the local bar. As she comes in, he says to the bartender, 'Now I remember what I was drinking to forget.'"*
Optimistic	**Pessimistic**
"Why did the girl put a clock under her pillow? So she would wake up on time."	*"Why did Robin Hood steal from the rich? Because the poor don't have any money."*
Strengthens personal bonds	**Disrupts personal relations**
"Definition of inverse paranoia: The belief that there are people out there in the world who are secretly trying to bring joy and happiness into your life."	*"I like knowing you 'cause knowing you proves there's someone even more pathetic than me."*
Results in feeling good	**Results in feeling bad**
"My dad's stories are so funny that I laugh before he tells them."	*"My mom's cooking is so bad, she puts barf bags next to the dinner plates instead of napkins."*
Likely to be enjoyed by others	**Likely to be hurtful to others**
"If your ship hasn't come in, swim out to it."	*"People who stutter never have to worry about their oral reports being too short."*

more uplifting and socially appropriate forms, especially in children. Hostile humor to some degree is unavoidable. What is avoidable is *excessively* hostile humor.

A hostile joke allows for the verbal expression of the aggressive drive, without actually striking someone. For example, *"Why don't you take a long walk off a short pier?"* To express aggression physically is dangerous and usually illegal (except in certain contact sports and wood chopping). In children, the problems with hostile humor typically arise with teasing (discussed on page 95), often with other kids present, or during excessive tickling by an adult to the point of discomfort in the child.

Personal Targets

Most joke forms have specific targets. Sometimes the targets are large institutions such as the government, the military, or society at large. No one person seems to be in danger of being hurt by becoming the butt of one of these jokes. However, in many forms of humor, there is a personal target, such as a homeroom teacher, Dad, or a friend. It's important to remind children that real people have real feelings.

How does your child think his friend Bob will feel if he says, "Bob is so dumb that he spells his name with two o's"? The comment may be clever, but it's also hurtful. In fact, the greatest risk for children's inappropriate use of personal targets in their humor is its negative effects on other kids. Adult authority figures are much less likely to feel personally wounded from kids' humor to the degree of actual psychological harm. Not so for kids, whose self-esteem and developing identities are most fragile. The scars and consequences of being the continual butt of jokes can have long-term effects.

A child who is the target of mean-spirited humor will remember the painful experience and be negatively affected by these events for a lifetime. For example, for a child to say to someone with an acne problem, "Did the weather report say whether you would have any facial clearing this weekend?" would be extremely cruel. There's a good chance that a child with such a skin problem is already very self-conscious, and that any jokes about the problem would only increase his self-consciousness. Such a comment is not likely to be forgotten—ever. Jokes made about a young girl's weight could actually predispose her to developing anorexia or bulimia in adolescence. She could become obsessed with her weight and adopt an unrealistic self-concept as an obese person. Similarly, a boy who is often made fun of about his allegedly short height or big nose could in adulthood suffer from the syndrome of body dysmorphic disorder—an intense preoccupation with some very minor or even nonexistent defect regarding a part of the body. At the very least, kids who are perpetual butts of childhood jokes frequently experience a lifetime of associated anxiety, poor self-esteem, and even clinical depression.

Clearly, most kids who use such humor do not intend to create such stress or psychological disorders in their "victims." Indeed, their jokes may be masking their own feelings of inferiority, insecurity, and inadequacy. Parents do not have to become amateur psychotherapists to deal with these issues. I simply advise parents to be alert to and discourage their kids' use of specific personal targets. It is so much better to use humor to "attack" more general targets, such as cafeteria food or a professional football team on a losing streak.

Practical Jokes

How can humor be physically harmful? Practical jokes frequently create humor through physical actions, such as pulling a chair out from under someone as she prepares to sit down. Another example would be hitting someone directly in the face with a chocolate cream pie, which could result in eye damage, broken glasses, or even bruises—not to mention expensive dry-cleaning costs. This may even seem funny for an instant, if at all, but the risks of real harm are too great. (For this reason, pie throwing should be reserved for slapstick comedies.)

Practical jokes can also involve contrived events. For example, someone might leave a wallet on the sidewalk at dusk with a difficult-to-see black thread attached to it. As an unsuspecting passerby reaches down to pick it up, the prankster pulls the thread so the wallet moves out of reach. Little obvious harm results in this case, other than the victim's embarrassment. Another example of a contrived event as a practical joke would be sending in the postage-paid cards to order numerous unwanted magazines in the name of a friend. Of course, this practical joke is hostile and creates unnecessary expenses and labor for companies and the postal service, all for an event of relatively little humor. As with most practical jokes, the perpetrator and associates, if any, derive much more pleasure than the victims.

Practical jokes can also be verbal. Many April Fools' Day jokes are verbal practical jokes. Sometimes they are elaborately contrived, but other times the joke has been set up quite simply. One or more people may be "in" on the joke in which some misinformation is provided to mislead the victim. Then, when the truth is suddenly revealed, usually to as large an audience as possible, the butt of the joke feels stupid or embarrassed. A practical joke in a classroom setting would have a built-in audience of thirty or more. Such a large crowd will usually heap more embarrassment on the victim than a smaller crowd would. No one likes to be the red-faced kid or teacher in the front of the class.

Very young children are not usually able to carry out elaborate practical jokes. The risk here is that if they observe such
humor carried out by adults as influential models, children may
think that this type of humor can be funny, even though cruel,
and will attempt it when they are better able to do so. On the
other hand, older preteen children are certainly capable of carry-
ing out practical jokes, like making phony phone calls to ask if
someone's refrigerator is running (and, if so, suggest they go
catch it). The humor here is minimal and based on a simple pun
("running"). While annoying and intrusive to the recipient of the
call, little actual harm is done. On the other hand, phony phone
calls made to the police or the fire department—false reports of
bombs or shots fired—are practical jokes with potentially expensive or dangerous consequences.

Sneaking up behind someone and squirting her with a water
gun is not funny to the victim. Even if she's not physically hurt,
she will feel a bit humiliated and certainly targeted. Have you
noticed that even in a swimming pool, where there is water
everywhere and people are dressed to get wet, no one seems to
enjoy being splashed in the face? Practical jokes are rarely very
funny and nearly always hostile and hurtful. Therefore, in the
presence of children, all practical jokes should be avoided.

Sex, "Dirty" Words, and Bathroom Humor

These topics can be funny to all of us within certain limits, but
they are almost always funny to kids with few if any limits. Just
saying certain words out loud without their even being a part of
a joke or comment sometimes seems hilarious to children.
Humor built upon sexual matters, "dirty" words, or bathroom
functions tends to crop up with kids frequently, but rarely is it
appropriate humor for or by children.

Sex has always been a taboo topic, more or less, in Western

societies. So, jokes involving sexual topics or words frequently are extraordinarily funny to most of us. The reason many jokes involve sex, according to Freud, is that such jokes allow the sex drive to be expressed in a non-biological form and in a relatively safe, socially approved way. That is, we can gratify our sexual urges without actually having sex. Is this good?

"Dirty" words are inappropriate because they allude to or refer to sex or bathroom functions. It must be confusing to growing children to first be told very clearly that jokes about sex are dirty, and later be told that sex is really a beautiful physical interaction that happens between two people who are in love (and, of course, legally married). This paradox recalls Woody Allen's famous observation that sex is not dirty unless you do it right.

As part of our socialization, we learn not to talk publicly about our normal biological bathroom functions. They are taboo, private, and presumably "dirty" activities. Consequently, children, trying to be funny, greatly enjoy bathroom-related jokes or just saying the names of those functions or the euphemisms for the body parts involved. Bathroom humor is a child's way of testing the limits of social acceptability. If parents get upset or embarrassed by that humor, the child has achieved a glorious and powerful victory in the generation wars without firing a single bullet.

Stereotypically Based Humor

Kids may learn very subtly from adults—sometimes, even from their parents—that it is okay to make fun of and laugh at certain groups of people. For example, the targets of their parents' humor may be certain religious groups, people from a different social class, or people speaking with different accents or of a different skin color. Through such humor, kids learn, without anyone ever saying so out loud, that it is just fine and acceptable to laugh at those who are in some way different from us. Maybe the target group has more money or possessions or less money and possessions. Maybe they have darker skin or lighter skin than we do. Maybe they follow different religious practices or none at all. Maybe they prefer to dress in fashions unlike our own.

The main point is that these kinds of differences among people should *never* be used as humor stimuli. They simply represent differences from our own group or are indicative of certain societal stereotypes. In all cases, adults should strongly discourage these forms of humor. It's not that such humor is never funny; it sometimes can be. Some professional comedians actually specialize in stereotypically based humor. But, most often, ethnic and racial forms of humor will be counterproductive to a socially constructive society and positive interpersonal relationships. Generally, it is safest to use a specific group as a humor target only when you yourself are a member of that group.

The Human Genome Project—a scientific study by the National Institutes of Health and U.S. Department of Energy—confirmed that humans and fruit flies are made up of a similar number of genes—30,000 or so. The Project concluded that all human beings are 99.9 percent alike. Certainly the racial and physical differences that do exist among humans are extremely trivial. No person or groups of people are superior to any other, and similarly, no person or groups of people could possibly deserve to be the butts of any ill-advised humor because they are "different" in *any* way. If we can promote this simple value in our children, we will have taken a major step forward in creating a society that is fair and fun for all.

Teasing and Taunting

Teasing involves a playful verbal attack on another person. It often begins in a humorous and affectionate way and is well accepted and enjoyable at that level, especially if it is done back and forth between "equals." However, teasing can easily escalate into a fairly aggressive act in which the humor, if it was ever present, gets lost entirely. And when the teasing is repeated frequently, even extending over days and weeks, it actually becomes abusive.

Taunting is a more verbally advanced form of teasing involving insulting sarcasm, mockery, and ridicule. Rarely does the target perceive any accompanying affection in taunting. In recent years, taunting has become so common in athletics that college football rules require that the entire team be penalized if a player engages in blatant taunting of an opponent. Both extreme teasing and taunting require a personal target, which was discussed on pages 90 to 91. Refer to that discussion to learn about the devastating effects this can have on an individual child.

What do I recommend instead? *Kidding.* The term "just kidding" is often mentioned to targets when the teasing and taunting produce negative reactions. I suggest that the kidding be clear and genuine from the beginning. True kidding is kind of affectionate ridicule, carried out playfully with no intent to humiliate. The "play signals" of smiling and a joking tone make it obvious to everyone that the comments are being made nonaggressively and purely for fun. (See page 82 in Chapter 5 for more on play signals.)

FEEDBACK ON NEGATIVE FORMS OF HUMOR

What should you do when your child tells a sex or bathroom joke or utilizes humor in any negative way? You can explain with a serious tone and attitude why you do not appreciate such humor and why most people will not like it. If the offense is very important to you, then a warning of future punishment may be a good idea. Make that punishment reasonable and not excessive. (We are referring, for example, to denial of dessert, an hour early to bed, or a short time in the "time out" area, *not* a slap in the face or soap in the mouth.) If your child persists or does it again, deliver the punishment as promised. Repeat this process as needed.

Part of the feedback session can be a slice of empathy training. Point out how hurt the target of the joke must feel, and ask your child how she would feel if their roles were reversed. (See the discussion on page 98 on promoting empathy.) This can be done in a very serious tone, while still praising your child's interest in and attempt at humor. Clearly, though, you must communicate that you do not tolerate hurtful humor.

It is necessary for parents to understand that when a child is taught that a particular form of humor is unacceptable at home and within the family, that same humor might be popular with the child's peers on the playground or at school. Bathroom and sexual humor and jokes targeting minorities are typical examples of this dilemma for parents. The child must learn to make a distinction based on the setting. At home, the joke or comment may not be approved; but with friends, it might get rewarded easily. Certainly make it clear to your child that you do not approve of such humor, but be aware that she may use it to be accepted by her peers.

What can your child do if her friend tells a joke that she has learned is not socially acceptable, or a joke that makes her feel uncomfortable? If your child is taught to say that the joke or comment is not "appropriate" or "nice," there's a good chance she will be shunned and even socially isolated by the other kids. The best strategy for dealing with humor that your child may find inappropriate is for her to *not* laugh, which fails to reward the humor abuser. Failure to garner a laugh from a joke or comment is a very powerful "non-reward." Then your child can move the conversation on to a new topic to minimize the attention to the unacceptable remarks. This is not an easy road to travel for children, or for many adults, because the esteem of a friend may be at stake. Nevertheless, the journey is worth it.

PROMOTING EMPATHY

Empathy is the ability to enter the world of another person without being influenced by your own attitudes and values. You see and feel things *as if* you were that other person, yet without losing the sense of your own identity. Empathy is a very desirable personal quality for successful therapists, great friends, and humor makers who try to minimize their use of hostile and negative humor.

You can foster empathic abilities in your child by helping her imagine how others might feel in certain situations. At first, the process will be primarily cognitive, as you and your child try to think of likely possibilities. Eventually, your child will experience feelings similar to those of a child who has been the target of a joke, although usually to a lesser degree. To the extent that your child can increase her empathic abilities, she will be less likely to tease others and to make them the target of hostile practical and verbal jokes.

For pure humor-making purposes, there is an interesting downside to empathy. If you feel *too* strongly on behalf of people in general—that is, if you are *overly* sensitive to the feelings of others—your own humor creation and performances could be inhibited. It is not always easy to establish that balance between appropriate levels of sentimentality and effective joking skills.

Children's literature expert Michael Cart agrees, "Empathy is one of humor's worst enemies. So is sentimentality. . . ." Some children may identify too closely with the butt of a joke, even if the targets are very much unlike themselves (such as a minority group member). This effect is both positive and negative. It is positive to be able to appreciate the probable feelings in another human being and to strive not to hurt others. It is negative because an *excess* of such sensitivity can eliminate many forms of humor expression and the enjoyment of humor. Certainly some specific jokes are highly inappropriate for children, but there will always be genuinely funny jokes about football players and mothers-in-law that we can enjoy and share, even though some unnamed football player or mother-in-law (rarely the same person) did not especially like the joke.

The highly empathic child will be very much aware that real people have real feelings, and will tend not to enjoy jokes at some real person's expense. Interestingly, the popular superiority theory of humor, discussed in Chapter 1, has trouble explaining this "problem." That theory would predict that one would especially enjoy such humor because someone else is the victim. By definition, the observer or listener would be feeling good because the trouble (the misfortune or humiliation) has happened to some other person.

Nevertheless, empathy is generally a good quality to have and to encourage in children. It makes humor creation a much more enjoyable practice for everyone involved.

POSITIVE AND NEGATIVE EFFECTS OF HUMOR

Professional clinical psychologist and amateur hospital clown Frank MacHovec described thirty-two separate possible effects that humor can create, although some of them may overlap. Of the total thirty-two consequences, he listed fifteen distinctly positive effects and *zero* negative effects on the person doing the humor making. When humor happened with one or more other people present, he found constructive and supportive effects, including lightening the mood, reducing anxiety, and facilitating intimacy and creativity. He judged that another eleven effects could be either positive or negative, such as defensively protecting oneself from attacks of reality or insincerely manipulating another person's feelings.

Dr. MacHovec believed that only two applications of humor are clearly offensive: the direct or indirect use of humor as a weapon. A direct attack would be the blatant use of humor to deliberately degrade or abuse another specific person. An indirect attack would be humor based on a prejudice against someone's race, age, ethnicity, religion, social status, or even occupation.

The important conclusion that we can draw from Dr. MacHovec's system is that there are many more probable positive uses of humor than possible negative uses. However, those negative uses of humor are powerful and can be tempting. If the target person's reactions are distress and outrage, the humor maker may attempt to defuse her anger by accusing her of being a poor sport. Those people who are most apt to use such negative humor are, in effect, keeping a kind of "get out of jail free" card in that way, refusing to accept responsibility for their harsh comments. The kidder then is able to express aggression through humor, to remain "superior" to the target of the humor, and to proclaim righteous innocence regarding the motivation for the humor. These complex social phenomena make it all the more critical to teach our children from the beginning that negative uses of humor are wrong, hurtful, and simply unacceptable.

CONCLUSION

As adults, we realize that sometimes so-called inappropriate humor is indeed funny. Humor that genuinely is racist, sexist, ageist, heterosexist, and so on can often be hilarious. That is why various amateur and professional humorists continue to produce it. Nevertheless, such humor can also be very hurtful.

The purpose of teaching your child how to develop her sense of humor is ultimately to build her self-esteem and a positive self-image, certainly not to destroy those qualities in other people. Thus, you need to be very alert to your child's humor efforts as she learns her humor skills. There will be errors, of course, as learning proceeds. But you can gently guide your child and model the kinds of humor you want to encourage. The result will be a pleasant addition to your child's personality that is guaranteed to be well received by her friends and family.

The next chapter discusses humor use by special needs children. The chapter you just read is helpful in teaching your child to respect the feelings of special needs children when their differences become apparent in social situations. So be sure to keep this chapter in mind as you read the next.

CHAPTER 7

Humor Use by Special Needs Children

*Emily has a delicious sense of humor. She is constantly
making word associations that are deep, meaningful and funny.
They seem to come out of nowhere. Over and over again she
will sum up a situation with a humorous comment, and we will
all laugh at the relationship she has seen and called to our attention.*

—J'ANNE ELLSWORTH, MOTHER OF SEVEN-YEAR-OLD EMILY,
WHO HAS DOWN SYNDROME

SOMETIMES IT'S EASY TO FORGET that *all* children can benefit from developing a sense of humor—no matter what challenges they face, whether it be a physical disability, Down syndrome, poor eyesight, or any one of a number of "special" circumstances. Many times we see only the obvious features and the possible limitations of children who are physically ill or in some way less able than others. Consequently, we may tend to treat these special needs children differently in terms of how we interact with them and what we expect from them. It doesn't have to be that way. As you will learn, most of the suggested activities and strategies in this book apply to these kids, too.

Many parenting books provide very little advice on special needs children. It's true that these children are statistically less common, but they are no less important and deserve, at least in this book, special mention. Therefore, this chapter is included for the parents of special needs children. But *all* parents should read this chapter for the useful information it contains—especially for helping their non-special needs child to interact positively with others despite their differences.

WHO ARE SPECIAL NEEDS CHILDREN?

We use the term "special needs children" here in the broadest possible sense. It includes both kids whose physical appearances define them as different and those kids who cannot be identified as "special" by casual observation, but are nonetheless "different" in some way. The former type includes kids with Down syndrome; kids who wear glasses, dental braces, or scoliotic appliances; kids who are significantly overweight, underweight, unusually tall, or very short; and kids with cerebral palsy, physical deformities, or other obvious limitations such as amputations, cleft palates, or crossed eyes. This particular type of special needs child requires ways to cope with stares, taunts, and directly cruel comments, which inevitably will happen, however unfortunate. Other children and even some adults may be apt to make insensitive remarks or ask thoughtless, hurtful questions. It is less likely that kids who are obviously very physically sick would be the butt of jokes, but that, too, could happen.

The latter type of special needs child cannot be identified without some personal interaction. These kids do not look different at first glance because their needs can be hidden or are not obvious. For example, kids who are dyslexic, mentally deficient, or emotionally disturbed; or have chronic physical illnesses, such as leukemia, AIDS, severe asthma, diabetes, or cystic fibrosis, have medical and psychological problems that generally do not affect their appearance. They usually look like all the other kids and attend school and after-school activities along with other kids. However, there's a good chance that their conditions will eventually become known to their peers in one way or another. At that point, these special needs kids could become the targets of teasing and cruel jokes, and therefore also need to learn coping devices—humor being one of them.

Most special needs kids, just like most other kids, can enjoy following the major league baseball standings, have trouble learning fractions, fall off skateboards, love Disneyland and spaghetti, play video games for hours, check out the latest fashions, listen to the hottest musicians on CDs or MTV, root for the closest pro football team, and look forward to birthday parties. In other words, special needs children are *children*, and they like the things that most kids like—including jokes and other forms of humor.

HUMOR STUDIES IN AUTISTIC AND DOWN SYNDROME CHILDREN

Child development researchers Paula St. James and Helen Tager-Flusberg of the University of Massachusetts at Boston conducted one of the few studies ever done on humor in autistic and Down syndrome children. During hour-long visits that took place over the period of a year, the researchers observed examples of humor by the children in their own homes, as the children played with their mothers in loosely structured activities.

The study included six boys with autism and four boys and two girls with Down syndrome who were matched to the autistic children in age and language abilities. The twelve children ranged in age from three years to six years. The researchers recorded humorous episodes, defined as the child's overt laughter, over and above mere smiling or excitement. They also noted whether or not the humor was socially based, that is, whether it was shared humor.

The major findings of this unique study were that *all* these special needs children (except one autistic child) demonstrated some incongruity humor in every session. The children with autism were capable of producing and appreciating humor, although they did so less often than the Down syndrome children. The vast majority of the humor produced by both groups of children was nonverbal—the only "formal" jokes that were told during the observation sessions were "knock-knock" jokes told by two of the Down syndrome children. It was found that all of the children with Down syndrome produced intentional humor, but only half of the autistic children's humor indicated any degree of purposefulness. Most of the autistic children's humor episodes were socially shared experiences, either responding to the mother's initiated humor, such as tickling (unlike these researchers, I do not consider tickling to be true humor), or getting the mother to respond to their humor initiatives. The autistic children were very much aware of how to violate the other person's expectations, which, indeed is the essence of how to produce humor.

Thus, despite what many people might expect at first, all these children with severe developmental disabilities did show humor. Clearly, more research is needed to understand the differences in the use and comprehension of humor in developmentally delayed children. Future studies must involve more children across a greater range of ages. We must give full credit to scientists St. James and Tager-Flusberg for conducting this pioneering research that validates our belief that these types of special needs children, too, can enjoy and produce humor.

Additional research at the University of Minnesota's Institute of Child Development compared the development of laughing and smiling between normally developing and Down syndrome infants, ages four to eighteen months. Although the special needs kids exhibited the humor behaviors on an average of seven months later than other children, the *order* of their occurrence was the same as with the cognitively normal infants: Smiling appeared before laughter, and laughter in response to auditory and tactile stimuli appeared before laughter in response to visual and social stimuli. The scientific evidence confirms that the development of the sense of humor in these special needs kids follows the same pattern as that of all kids, only a bit more slowly.

WHAT PARENTS OF SPECIAL NEEDS KIDS SHOULD KNOW ABOUT HUMOR DEVELOPMENT

Parental expectations are especially important. Too often, parents of special needs kids have been mistakenly told of the likely extreme limitations of their children by misguided health-care workers. For example, they may say that the child will never be normal, should be institutionalized, or will have no personality. More often than not, these professionals are mistaken. In some cases, humor in special needs kids will be slower to develop, but it definitely can happen. In cases in which a child's disability is more physical, humor can develop as rapidly as in any other kid, but could also be delayed because others (wrongly) perceive the child to be mentally different and less capable. Parents are in unique positions to monitor their child and to communicate their expectations that humor appreciation and creation are very much anticipated.

Humor training for special needs kids in most ways should

follow the recommendations we made earlier: encourage humor appreciation, model the use and enjoyment of humor yourself, generously reward all appropriate humor efforts, and do fun things together, especially activities that have no purpose other than the pure pleasure of doing them. In this aspect of humor training, there are no special tricks or procedures for parents to use other than exhibiting greater patience in developing humor in an intellectually challenged child. Of course, when parents have a variety of problems to contend with, patience is more easily requested than achieved. Parents can and should turn to community support groups for help in this area. In addition, I strongly recommend reading Joseph A. Michelli's book *Humor, Play & Laughter*, which focuses on the use of humor to cope with the challenges of parenting.

HUMOR AS A COPING DEVICE FOR SPECIAL NEEDS CHILDREN

While well-adjusted adults tend to value differences among people and behavior, kids tend to place great value on conformity in appearance, conduct, and attitudes. When another kid seems to be different, he often becomes a target for abusive humor. Humor making can help targets of abusive humor—who unfortunately include many special needs children—cope with being teased and taunted because of their differences.

Having been victims, perpetrators, and witnesses of teasing and taunting at one time or another in our lives, we can all relate to this type of behavior, which, incidentally, more likely represents aggressive humor than helpful humor. We should all be aware that being teased and taunted can be upsetting and traumatic to the target. Therefore, the use of coping humor by special needs kids is perhaps even more critical for them than it is for most other kids. Be assured that special needs children can learn humor techniques—specifically self-effacing humor and defense-less humor—to cope with their special circumstances. Of course, they can also use humor in general to earn the acceptance and friendship of their peers. These techniques are discussed below. It might be interesting for children to know that many actors and comedians actually developed or used their sense of humor this way. See "'Special Needs' Famous People" on page 110, which discusses several well-known entertainers who not only used humor as a coping tool, but, in many cases, used it as the basis for a sucessful career.

Self-Effacing Humor

Humor training of healthy kids involves teaching them *not* to use cruel humor with any of the special needs kids that may be a part of their social worlds at school or in the neighborhood. Humor training by parents of special needs kids, though, must involve two goals: teaching their special needs kids that some self-effacing humor will be helpful and adaptive because it will defuse the power of those prone to make fun of them, and ex-plaining that too much self-effacing humor will backfire, if they too readily take on the role of a humor target. There is a delicate line between advocating humor use as a desirable personal trait and actually reinforcing the cruel humor of others. Self-effacing humor can help to solidify friendships and to acknowledge the special condition of the child, but such humor clearly must be used in moderation.

What exactly is self-effacing humor? Self-effacing humor does not put down anyone other than the speaker himself. It is safe, humble, and non-threatening. When a special needs child openly admits his differences and makes fun of them himself, there is no advantage left to others. Yes, he really *is* different from

"Special Needs" Famous People

Many professional comedians and actors talk about how they learned to use humor as a child to cope with their physical limitations. There are quite a number of examples; the following are just a few of them: Comedian Gerri Jewell capitalizes on her cerebral palsy as her primary comedic persona, and actor Michael J. Fox credits his childhood sense of humor with helping him avoid getting regularly beaten up by other kids, all of whom were significantly taller than he. Not only short in stature but also born with a clubfoot, British actor and comedian Dudley Moore admits to "retreating" into comedy to compensate for his physical deficiencies. And, although it is not widely known, television and movie star Bruce Willis stuttered as a child. As a result, he developed his excellent sense of humor to cope with the teasing he received from other children. And now he no longer stutters! Comedic actor Nathan Lane used humor to counter the traumas of being an overweight child living in a dysfunctional home with an alcoholic father. He recalls, "I was overweight as a kid, and being funny was a way of deflecting people making fun of me by

most other kids in this particular way, and that's okay for him to admit in a humorous way—and, of course, in serious ways, too.

Defenseless Humor

One particularly useful skill for special needs children to acquire is called *defenseless humor*. It can also be used by younger children to help them get along or peacefully coexist with older teasing bullies. In defenseless humor, a child uses a joke or other form of humorous comment in a clearly playful, but not demeaning, way. For example, a child who is being teased about his size making jokes before they could. It was part of my escape from a very difficult situation at home."

The famous cartoonist John Callahan, paralyzed from an auto accident at age twenty-one, has transformed his physical disability into a prolific career in humor by writing books and drawing cartoons that focus on disability and other taboo topics. In addition, he recently began a new animated series *Pelswick* on the Nickelodeon network, whose star is described by the network as "a fearlessly funny thirteen-year-old boy who happens to be in a wheelchair."

Parents can use this information about how these and other celebrities have overcome their "handicaps" to succeed in their chosen fields of comedy, acting, or writing. It would be most helpful if the example chosen matched the child in the area of disability. Certainly, the general concepts of overcoming obstacles with hard work, special training, and capitalizing on your own strengths are important lessons for all children. Another valuable message is that you can be very successful in your work and in your personal life *without* ever becoming rich and famous. Fame and money are not true measures of success for any of us.

might say something like, "Yes, you really are bigger and stronger than me. That is why I am making you my official bodyguard. This is quite an honor." It simply acknowledges the power differential and makes no attempt to retaliate or change anyone's status. Defenseless humor, when successful, makes a friend from an enemy. We realize that this particular example might be difficult or awkward for some kids because it uses unfamiliar phrasing. Parents can help create clever strategies in more familiar terms that their own kid can try, depending on the unique situations that have arisen.

Practicing Self-Effacing and Defenseless Humor

Kids can get so frustrated and angry when they are teased that they cannot quickly think of witty replies or methods to cope in these situations. It can help immensely for parents and older siblings to role-play with the special needs child to provide some examples of reasonable responses that can be made to other kids' taunts. By creating scenarios together, you and your child will be able to generate the kinds of words that best fit your child's particular situation.

When kids are convinced that this strategy will work, and they have some possible "comebacks" readily available, they will then feel confident enough to try out some of the suggested retorts. A possible alternative, which can be modified by parents as appropriate for their children, is saying something like, "I know I can't play this game because of my asthma, but I'm happy to keep score for everyone and cheer you on." Another alternative would be for a child who uses a wheelchair and consequently gets left out of physical games to offer to race an able-bodied child in a different wheelchair.

General Humor

Of course, special needs kids need not limit their expressions of humor to the self-effacing and defenseless types. Those forms of humor can help them gain acceptance from more able kids who may have started off being cruel or rejecting, but all of the usual forms of humor—jokes, riddles, and crazy props—are definitely recommended for special needs kids, too.

TEACHING CHILDREN TO INCLUDE SPECIAL NEEDS KIDS IN THEIR ACTIVITIES

Parents should be aware of the possibility that their children without special needs will have contact with special needs children, daily or less often. Either way, their children should know how to act appropriately with these kids. In Chapter 6, we discussed how humor can be abused by children. Ridiculing or humiliating special needs children with jokes and comments are examples of the inappropriate use of humor. We respectfully advise you to monitor your child closely to ensure that he is not a perpetrator of such unfair and cruel humor.

When it comes to special needs children, teasing is not the only concern. All too often, children with special needs are excluded from fun activities because of their differences, even when those differences would not interfere with a given activity. Keeping this in mind, you and your child can talk about what it means to be "different" and how it must feel to have a particular disease or disability and to be treated differently—regardless of whether your specific problem is relevant in a particular situation. For example, there is no reason a physically handicapped child can't participate in joke-sharing sessions or discussions of funny TV shows. There is no reason that a mentally challenged child could not enjoy being a part of the social group watching a funny movie or laughing at circus clowns. Even if the child does not contribute verbally to a discussion, just being present with everyone else and laughing at examples of humor will give that child a clear feeling of being accepted and included socially, as well as enhanced self-esteem. Going out with siblings and friends to a puppet show or funny movie can be great fun for *all* kids. There will be no test later. If any jokes or subtle humor is missed, it's okay. Everyone had fun and will want to go again.

SPOTTING HUMOR AT THE DOCTOR'S OFFICE

Special needs kids may spend more time in hospitals or doctors' offices than other kids. They will have unusual opportunities to spot humor that other people do not have. For example, the doctor's tongue depressor can be called an "ah stick" because that is what the doctor asks you to say when he puts the wooden stick in your mouth. An older child might jokingly ask the doctor why he must always be the one to take off his clothes, while the doctor never does. (This is a good question for adult patients to ask, too.) Or, "Why do surgeons make their patients sit on 'butcher' paper?" When preparing for an x-ray, patients are sometimes told to "strip to the waist, please." A humorous comment might be, "From which direction?" And, "If these x-rays are so safe, why does everyone else leave the room?"

Kids with cancer undergo a number of unpleasant experiences as part of their medical diagnosis and treatments. They are likely to lose their hair, feel extreme nausea and fatigue, and perhaps have difficulty sleeping. Research evidence suggests that those kids who use humor to cope with negative experiences, called "cancer stressors," tend to develop fewer infections and achieve better psychosocial adjustments to their illness. Partly due to this research, nurses assigned to pediatric cancer wards are encouraged to use humor deliberately in their daily work with young patients.

More and more hospitals in America are recognizing the value of humor in providing total care for their patients. Many now feature Humor Rooms or Humor Carts, which can be brought to patients in their rooms. The humor rooms or carts contain a variety of comedy tapes, humor books and magazines, joke books, funny novels, games, and endless props for humor making. Patients can choose whichever items interest them. At the very least, these items become pleasant distractions from the boring and often painful experiences of being treated in a hospital. At the most, they represent vital avenues to attitudinal changes and potent pathways to actual healing. The research evidence is still coming in on the efficacy of humor for healing, but in the meantime, why not offer humor materials to medical patients, especially children, to enhance their quality of life in difficult circumstances?

The movie *Patch Adams* described the true story of a renegade physician named Hunter "Patch" Adams, played by Robin Williams, who believes in using humor as a medical therapy. While most practicing physicians vigorously retain their stereotypical image of serious (humorless) professionals, Dr. Adams is not above dressing as a gorilla or filling a hospital room with balloons or a bathtub with noodles to bring some healing humor to his patients. Incidentally, he received his M.D. despite being officially chastised in medical school for his "excessive happiness."

Some pediatric dentists and child psychologists are incorporating humor into their practices on a limited basis, primarily to reduce anxiety in their young patients. They might wear a funny tie or a colorful fright wig, and stock their waiting room with lots of toys and funny posters. These professionals are indeed the exceptions. We should reward them by praising them and patronizing them (but not in a demeaning way).

CONCLUSION

This chapter on special needs children was written for two main reasons: to emphasize that these children typically will need especially well-developed humor skills to cope with teasing and bullies; and to remind parents that the very same techniques used to develop humor skills in the average child will also work with the special needs child.

Other than their particular disability or illness, the special needs child is like all others. These children can benefit enormously by developing a sense of humor and can make special use of their humor talents for social coping. They can become not just "one of the kids," but kids who are sought out for their personal friendliness and fun.

CHAPTER 8

Jest for Teachers
(& Parents, Too)

Humor belongs in the classroom—
for what it teaches us and for its own sake.

—VINCENT ROGERS, EDUCATION PROFESSOR

KIDS SPEND MORE HOURS EACH DAY in school than they do waking hours at home. Moreover, they are receiving formal instruction earlier and earlier in their lives—many children are enrolled in preschool when only three years old! Teachers, therefore, have an enormous influence on the social and personal development of our children. That's why this chapter is devoted to them. But parents, too, can benefit from reading this chapter—and will probably even want to share what they learn with their children's teachers.

Of course, no discussion of humor in the classroom would be complete without a discussion of class clowns, so this chapter starts with one. Then, it goes on to discuss the importance of humor in the classroom before focusing on specific exercises that teachers can use with their students. This chapter concludes with a description of an innovative humor program that is ongoing at

Murdock Elementary School in La Mesa, California. After reading about it, I hope that other schools will want to offer a similar program to their students.

CLASS CLOWNS

Class clowns have always been the nemesis of classroom teachers from kindergarten to college. With their well-developed sense of humor, these kids have acted up in class to the delight of their classmates ever since formal education moved indoors. Class clowns learn early how to exploit the *social contagion principle* of laughter—that the presence of other people facilitates the expression of laughter. Laughter is more intense and lasts longer when others are present. Classmates become the best possible audience, and the classroom is a perfect setting for contagious laughter. Very bright kids who are easily bored with the standard lessons or those kids who have difficulty maintaining their attention for long periods are typically the ones who become class clowns. Being a class clown allows these students to achieve a positive level of social status that they might not be able to attain through academic means.

Many, if not most, professional comedians had been the class clowns in their youthful school days. Jonathan Winters, Dennis Miller, Robin Williams, and Richard Lewis are prominent examples. Steve Allen described himself as having been "a moderately decorous class clown" because without becoming disruptive to the class, he would give comic answers to his teachers' serious questions. Boys are more likely than girls to take on the role of class clown. A prominent exception is comedic actress Jennifer Aniston, who was a class clown in high school.

As we all know, longstanding traditions in education have placed a premium on a well-ordered, quiet, and serious setting for learning. So quite often, these funny kids are punished by teachers who do not approve of such humorous attention-attracting antics in school. This atmosphere trains students to suppress their natural inclinations toward humor rather than exploit those interests toward greater learning. It doesn't have to be this way.

Like parents, teachers must realize that a sense of humor in children is a highly desirable personal characteristic. Kids with a keen sense of humor will likely be more creative, more assertive, and better adjusted. Those budding class clowns' jokes and pranks can actually be harnessed for the enjoyment of all. The exercises beginning on page 123 will give you some idea how to go about doing this. Also, see the inset "Class Clown Competition" on page 121 for an additional innovative approach to harnessing humor-making talent in students.

When the unofficially designated class clown or any other student spontaneously says something funny, what can a teacher do? First, she can explicitly acknowledge that the comment was funny by laughing and even saying so. If it is important to return to the lesson, the teacher should do so firmly and quickly, perhaps reminding the class to store up their funny comments for a class time designated for verbal silliness or comedy. It is important for the teacher *not* to lose control of the learning environment or to draw excessive attention to the clown. Laugh, but move on immediately. While the class clown's comments may have drawn laughs, the teacher needs to redirect the class and to be quite clear that the remarks are out of order *at this time,* but that there will be another time when such humor will be truly appreciated.

All social behaviors have an appropriate time and place. This maxim is true for humor making as well. We want to encourage the humor of class clowns and all its associated positive characteristics, while discouraging clowning—not punishing it—in the actual academic class.

If you are a parent who is fortunate enough to have a class clown for a child, you can feel genuinely proud that you have successfully encouraged your child's development of a sense of humor; that your child is also likely to be very verbal, intelligent, and creative; and that your child is already comfortable speaking and performing in public. Successful professionals in many fields—business managers, teachers, lawyers, physicians, landscape architects, engineers, public relations professionals, and others—must have competent public-speaking skills to make effective presentations to groups of all sizes. For most people, this task generates extreme anxiety. Your child knows no such fear and is ready to perform comfortably in any business, not just show business.

Of course, some old-fashioned teachers may be less sympathetic to the positive aspects of having a class clown in class, and may complain. It is unlikely that you will be able to change the views of this kind of teacher. The best strategy in this case is to agree that class disruptions by your child are not appropriate, and that you will gladly work with the teacher to redirect the child's humor efforts toward better outlets. If there are opportunities within your child's school, such as a drama club, a speech-making club, or a comedy competition team, that would be ideal. If not, there may be relevant community resources that could be tapped, such as junior theater and improv classes for kids.

INCORPORATING HUMOR IN THE CLASSROOM

Many scientific studies have confirmed that when humor is part of a classroom lesson or demonstration, students are more likely to retain the information being taught. They attend to the points

class clown competition

What can a teacher do to harness a class clown's natural inclination to make others laugh? Well, Australia features a national class clown competition for students ages nine to twelve. After competing in several regional rounds, the winners are invited to perform standup routines or comedy skits and songs at the finals at the Melbourne International Comedy Festival each year. Cash prizes are awarded to the winners and to their schools. This opportunity provides an excellent and socially appropriate outlet for those budding comedy talents that tend to show up first in elementary school classrooms.

Since the United States does not yet have a comparable program, a motivated teacher could first initiate a class clown competition in her school, and then perhaps arrange a competition against one or more neighboring schools. Local Toastmasters International Clubs might be willing to help the school by sponsoring the meets, and to aid in judging the kids' performances. Comedy contests clearly are safer than interscholastic football and more fun than a chess club tournament.

more closely and enjoy being present in the class. There is little doubt of the basic educational value of incorporating humor in both formal and informal classroom activities. Yet laughter in the classroom is still too rare.

Humor can easily be incorporated into traditional curricular topics. For example, mental arithmetic problems for very young children in the early grades can involve well-known characters, such as Barney or Elmo. You could say, "Barney had six *apples* and gave four of them to Elmo. How many *oranges* did Barney have left?" Of course, no one knows how many *oranges* Barney had. That's what makes it funny. We can figure out, however, that Barney has two apples left. That's what makes it educational. Also, language lessons can involve defining puns and making some up, even in the early primary grades. The students can be engaged in discovering how words that sound the same can mean very different, frequently funny, things. For example, *"When super glue was invented, lots of kids became attached to it!"* Older students can be assigned comedy plays or humorous poems to read and critique. History lessons can include various illustrations of United States presidential humor, such as the spontaneous witticisms of President Kennedy in his press conferences. Creative writing assignments can call for students to write original jokes, riddles, puns, or satires on current events. Other examples include class discussions, art projects, and classroom contests centered on humor; monthly or weekly humor days when everyone brings in a funny joke or cartoon to share with the group; and field trips to places like the zoo, where the kids can imitate the animals. When teachers use their imaginations, the opportunities to incorporate humor into the classroom are virtually endless.

Professor of Education Vincent Rogers urges teachers to nurture humor vigorously in their classrooms by encouraging and demonstrating those personal qualities of a humorous perspective presented by clinical psychologist Harvey Mindess. (These six personal qualities were discussed on pages 11 through 14 of Chapter 1.) Rogers adds, "Good teachers, then, are prepared to laugh at *themselves,* to share their own mistakes, to help children understand that teachers, too, are human. Good teachers also encourage their students to laugh at themselves, to relieve tension by allowing themselves to see the occasional absurdities, inconsistencies, and sometimes just plain foolishness in their day-to-day behavior."

If teachers freely use humor and reward humor efforts, their students will have a wonderful opportunity to develop a sense of humor, and overall learning will be facilitated. Their kids will definitely be "kids who laugh"!

CLASSROOM HUMOR EXERCISES

As we all know, school is a place for learning. Not only do kids learn in formal ways through lessons in math, science, history, and so on, but they also learn a great deal informally by observing and interacting with their teachers and fellow students. Planned humor activities in which all the students are involved can give children the opportunity to learn humor skills from one another, while receiving structured guidance from their teachers.

Modern and progressive teachers (that is, those reading this book) are very aware that humor enhances learning. It makes for an enjoyable and accepting classroom environment in which students are stimulated to explore ideas, to think in unusual ways, and to consider different perspectives on issues. Claudia Cornett's book *Learning Through Laughter: Humor in the Classroom* identifies thirteen reasons why humor is important for students. We hope that you need no more convincing of the value of humor as part of formal education and as a major tool in your own teaching bag of tricks.

Offered below are some concrete exercises for encouraging humor in the classroom from preschool to sixth grade. Of course, you as a teacher should tailor these suggestions to the academic, developmental, and social levels of the students in your class. Some of the ideas for the earlier grades might also be fun for kids in the later grades. The suggestions for the later grades, however, might be too involved for younger students. But please read all of the suggested exercises because many of them can be adapted to any age. They can be carried out exactly as described, or they can be modified to fit the day's lesson plan—as a teacher, you know which activities your students will respond to and enjoy most. I also encourage you to use your imagination and come up with your own humor-filled ideas!

EXERCISES FOR PRESCHOOL AND KINDERGARTEN

Clay

Have the class create funny things from clay like clown faces or animals with exaggerated body parts, such as ears or tails. Use prepared clay or make your own by mixing white school glue with liquid starch and a few drops of food coloring until it has the consistency of malleable clay. (Or use any other clay recipe you may have seen in an arts and crafts book.)

Funny Costumes (or Pre-Halloween Day)

Have the students dress up in funny costumes sometime in the spring. (You can wear a funny costume, too!) To plan this properly, give the parents prior notice to obtain their necessary cooperation. On any day other than Halloween, they may not take their kids' requests to dress up in costumes seriously without word from you.

While most lessons will proceed as usual, even while in costume, at the end of the day, there can be a contest with candy prizes for the funniest costume, the most original costume idea, and so on.

Pictures

Have the kids draw pictures of what they think is funny. While they are drawing, walk around the classroom and ask each of them to tell you what she thinks is comical about her particular drawing. Hang the finished pictures around the classroom for everyone to see.

Show and Tell

Have kids bring in something that they think is funny to share with the class during show and tell—it could be a toy, a picture, a comic book, or whatever.

Story Time

Read a funny book to the class. When you read a part that's particularly humorous, stop and ask the class if they think it's amusing, too. See if they can tell you why. Try also stopping at parts that aren't so funny, and see what the kids say when you ask if that passage is comical.

Surprise the Kids

One day, wear a wig to school or something you wouldn't normally wear, like a funny hat or a pair of silly glasses. See how long it takes the kids to notice and begin to giggle. Pretend for a little while that you don't know what's amusing, but then let them in on the joke. You can also keep these props in the classroom and use them in front of the class occasionally. For example, you can unexpectedly don a pair of "Groucho Marx" glasses or a plastic red nose.

EXERCISES FOR FIRST AND SECOND GRADES

Friday Fun Time

Schedule time each week—Fridays are a good day for this—when each member of the class takes a turn telling a joke or posing a riddle to the class. There are many sources for easy jokes and riddles—the Internet, family and friends, books or magazines, and so on—or kids can come up with their own. Have some written ones handy for anyone who is unprepared. The main idea is for each student to participate by taking a turn sharing humor.

Humor-Creativity Game

Ask an open-ended question that requires responses which are both creative and humorous. Some examples are, *"What funny things can we do with old tennis balls?"* and *"How can you make someone laugh without speaking or touching that person?"*

Humor-Filled Classroom Environment

Create a humor-filled classroom environment by posting cartoons, funny sayings, witty quotations, silly photos, and the like all around the room. Invite students to bring these items from home to contribute to classroom fun. If your walls are already full of art projects and reports, establish a special humor bulletin board somewhere in the classroom. Students can have access to the board during breaks, and before and after regular class hours. This is a good example of something that would work well not only with young kids, but with older students, too.

Laughs on Command

Have laughter moments during class when everyone stops what they're doing and laughs on command—with no joke or specific humor stimulus. You can begin the laughter experience by laughing aloud and then nod to the first student to join in, who then nods to the next student, and so on. Soon, it will become a very raucous and healthful activity yielding all the physical benefits of humor-induced laughter. Along these same lines, you can also play the "Ho Ho Ha Ha" game. With no humor stimulus at all, you begin by saying, "ho ho ha ha," and then have each student, in turn, say "ho ho ha ha." This game takes just a minute or two, and will soon have everyone laughing spontaneously. Laughter will quickly relax the students, and they will be ready for formal class work.

A Real Clown in Class

Invite a clown in full costume to your classroom—even though the class may already include a number of untrained clowns. Ask the clown to discuss what it means to be a clown and how clowning is used to cheer up kids in hospitals. Different clowns will specialize in different forms of humor, including singing funny songs, doing magic tricks, telling jokes, or creating balloon animals. It's important to note that some very young children may be frightened by clowns, who may come across to them as loud, boisterous, or dangerous. Kids should be prepared for the clown's visit by a brief discussion beforehand about how the clown may look and act in outrageous and unusual ways and why clowns act that way.

Telephone Game

Play the telephone game to illustrate humorous communication failures. In this game, all the children line up, and you whisper a message into the ear of the first child. That child, in turn, passes on the message by whispering it to the child next to her, and this continues down the line. (Note that the kids can whisper the messages only once—no repeats allowed.) The last child in line gets to say the message aloud to the entire class. To everyone's delight, the final message will be very different from the original one.

The content and complexity of the original message should vary according to the ages of the children, but in all cases, it can be humorous. For example, the original message could be *"A tall man in a short hat walked under a low bridge knockin' his noggin."* Sometimes a tongue twister, such as *"A tutor who tooted a flute tried to tutor two tooters to toot,"* works very well in the telephone game.

EXERCISES FOR THIRD AND FOURTH GRADES

April Fools' Day

One week before April Fools' Day, have your class decide the best way to celebrate that special humor-filled day. Traditionally, April Fools' Day pranks involve practical jokes. This may be a good opportunity for you to conduct a discussion of possible abuses of humor and concerns for "victims" of harmful practical jokes. Have your students find better ways to celebrate this day. If they come up with many good ideas, a vote may be necessary to decide which ideas to use.

Brainstorming Games

Play creative brainstorming games. Brainstorming is a group activity and problem-solving exercise in which *all* ideas are welcome on a given topic. In most social situations, people edit and censor their ideas before speaking them aloud. However, in brainstorming, you will generate more innovative ideas when the participants are encouraged to eliminate all evaluative considerations. That is, don't worry about whether your contribution is good or bad, too expensive or too impractical, or too anything. Just explain your idea, and maybe someone else will be stimulated to add a new wrinkle or variation that will ultimately be even better—in this case, funnier. For instance, the class could try to come up with ideas about how the world would be different if we really did have our eyes in the back of our heads (as some teachers claim to have), or how school would be more fun, but still educational, if kids could make all the rules and lesson plans.

Daily Humor Sharing

You may want to begin or end each day (or week) with humor sharing. In this exercise, each child tells the whole class about something funny that happened. Stock jokes and riddles are permitted here, but students' observations of real events should be encouraged.

Exaggerations

Have the class create extreme exaggerations. You can start by saying, "The clown was so funny that . . ." or "The cat was so crazy that . . ." or "The elephant was so big that . . ." The students can then fill in the rest of the sentence with unrealistic, but funny, endings.

Humor Test

Create your own humor test by providing several one-frame cartoons from newspapers or magazines without their captions. Then give the kids a list of captions, and ask them to match the correct text with the correct cartoon.

Humorous Speechmaking Behaviors

As part of a lesson in oral presentations, model negative speechmaking behaviors—monotone, frequent pauses, and striking lack of enthusiasm. For example, the frequently heard statement from boring speakers, "I am very thrilled to be here today" can be delivered in a slow style with no inflection. These examples will be not only humorous but also informative.

Outlaw Humor

Discuss as a group what the world would be like if humor were outlawed. What would happen to all the funny things in the world—things like books, television shows, movies, and so on? Would people create humor secretly? What would the punishment be if you were caught being funny?

Photo Captions

Hold up large photos from magazines or newspapers that were not originally intended to be funny, and have the class come up with funny captions for them.

Share Your Blunders Game

Begin by telling a true embarrassing or silly thing that you said or did. Then ask volunteers to share one of their blunders with the class. (No child need share a personal blunder if she doesn't feel comfortable doing so.) This exercise teaches that it is okay to laugh at yourself, and that those temporary slips and gaffes can later seem funny.

Sounds and Words

Use humor-related activities and riddles to encourage the students to attend to critical aspects of language, such as the positioning of sounds within words and how words are put together. For example, *"Which two letters of the alphabet, when together, contain nothing? M-T."* or *"Why is the letter K like a pig's tail? Because it comes at the end of pork."*

Watch a Classic Comedy

Show a classic comedy film to the class and then discuss what was funny in the film and why. Excellent choices would be any of the Abbott and Costello, Marx Brothers, Charlie Chaplin, or Laurel and Hardy films. Even "modern classics" such as *Toy Story* or *Monsters, Inc.* can be considered for this exercise.

EXERCISES FOR FIFTH AND SIXTH GRADES

Bumper Stickers

Ask the students to pay attention to bumper stickers or personalized license plates for one week. At the end of the week, have them share some of the funnier ones they read with the class. Of course, not all of these public messages are intended to be humorous. For example, there's a bumper sticker that says the driver's child had been declared citizen of the week at his or her particular school. As a retort, there's a bumper sticker that says, "My child beat up the citizen of the week." Although this may be funny, it's not appropriate.

Daffynitions

Create some "daffynitions"—humorous definitions of common words. For example, "Shopping" is a kind of therapy that doesn't involve telling your secrets to anyone. "Diet" is a brief period of starvation usually followed by a gain of ten pounds. "School" is a place where children go while their parents take a daily vacation. "History" is the account of the accomplishments of men. (For women, the word would be "herstory.") Have the students come up with their own daffynitions as a group activity.

Humor Diary

Ask students to keep a diary of funny things they observe or experience for one week. At the end of the week, students can take turns reading some of their more amusing diary entries to the rest of the class.

Humor Lesson

Teach a class lesson on the subject of humor. It could fit into the English or social studies curriculum. Sample topics include the following: the theory that humor promotes health and a speedy recovery from illness; the major types of humor; varying humor preferences; how certain kinds of humor can be hurtful; how something that seems bad now can later seem funny; and how humor can help us cope with stress.

Humor Surveys

Have your students take a humor survey by asking ten people they know a question such as "What is your favorite joke?" or "What is the first joke you remember telling?" The students can write up reports on their findings and present their results to the class.

Humorous Speech Contest

Have the students prepare humorous speeches and hold a contest in which each child has one minute to read her speech to the class. A prize for the winner could be an inexpensive joke book or something else equally rewarding. The class can use a secret ballot to vote on the funniest speech.

Report on a Comedian

As a writing assignment, ask the students to choose their favorite comedian and discuss why that person is so appealing to them. It will make them think about why they find that person's humor so funny.

Report on a Comedy

Assign a written report on a situation comedy or a funny movie. What better reason for watching television or a movie could students possibly give their parents?

School Jokes Catalog

Have students bring in jokes that have to do with school situations, and write them in a book that you have designated as the "School Jokes Catalog"—a loose-leaf binder would be best so that the pages can be rearranged (or photocopied). The exercise can be expanded to teach students about indexing, alphabetization, cataloging, and other journalistic tasks. These jokes will be great fun to reread at the end of the term. Here's an example of a "school joke": *"A girl came home from her first day at school. Her mother asked, 'What did you learn today?' The girl replied, 'Not enough. They want me to come back tomorrow!'"*

Spoonerisms and Oxymorons

Define and illustrate humorous examples of spoonerisms or oxymorons. Spoonerisms are credited to the English clergyman Reverend W. A. Spooner, who often unintentionally interchanged the first sounds of words with a resulting humorous effect. For example, "funny bone" could be changed into the spoonerism "bunny phone," or "jelly beans" could become "belly jeans." Spoonerisms are funniest when they are spoken unintentionally and create a meaningful and humorous effect.

Similarly, our everyday world is filled with concepts that are actual oxymorons—mutually contradictory concepts, such as "jumbo shrimp" or "mandatory options" for your car. One of the terms in an oxymoron is humorously inconsistent with the other. Some additional examples, especially apt for children, are "healthy chocolate," "sad clown," "larger half," "play school," and "modern history." Many adults might add "working vacation" and "rap music."

Tom Swifties

A Tom Swifty is a play on words that creates a humorous effect by the punning relationship between the speaker's message and the adverb used to describe the speaker himself. Tom Swift was a literary character created by author Edward Stratemeyer, writing as Victor Appleton. Tom never said anything simply without a modifying adverb.

Define and illustrate Tom Swifties for your class and lead an exercise in creating more examples. Some examples could be *"I know who turned out the lights," Tom commented darkly. "I need a pencil sharpener," Tom said bluntly. "I don't like hot dogs," Tom complained frankly. "I can't steer my bicycle," Tom said straightforwardly. "I can't believe I ate the whole pineapple," Tom said Dolefully.* Students will have to possess fairly well-developed language skills to carry out this exercise. Once they get the hang of it, though, they're sure to enjoy themselves.

AN INNOVATIVE APPROACH TO LEARNING HUMOR AT SCHOOL

Murdock Elementary School in La Mesa, California has developed an innovative way of teaching humor. This school offers a Clown Club as one of its standard after-school activities. A parent, who is an amateur clown and classroom aide, directs the club, which meets for three different sessions of eight weeks each throughout the year. The kids learn how to apply clown makeup and costuming, and stage performances and skits at school. Dressed as clowns, they even visit local senior centers and convalescent patients. Interestingly, the Clown Club attracts a number of kids who ordinarily are quite shy and reserved, as well as more exuberant and lively kids.

What a great example of how to learn and use humor while making public service contributions. We take off our big plastic red noses in salute to the Murdock School Clown Club!

CONCLUSION

The ability to make people laugh may be the greatest gift anyone can have. And the opportunity to encourage that gift in children, our country's greatest natural resource, is truly most special. No

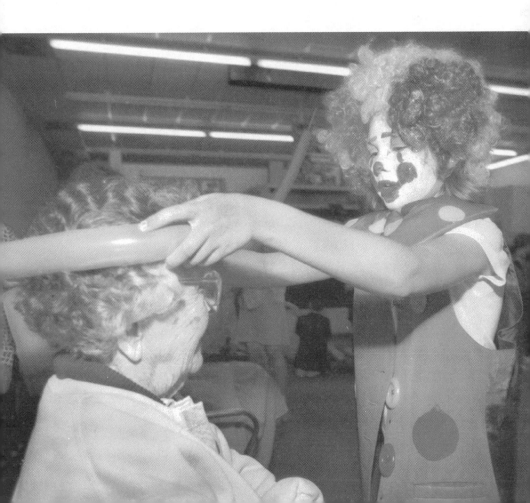

longer will a classroom in which laughter is heard be thought of as "out of control." Instead, these rooms will be ones where fun-loving teachers educate and fun-loving kids learn (and laugh).

Kids who enjoy going to school because it is a fun place will ultimately learn more in their classes. Their sense of humor will not be stunted but rather developed, and they will be more pleasant people as a result. We can confidently predict that absenteeism will be down in classes where humor is up. Teachers, please seize the opportunity so that every one of your students will laugh all the way from nursery school to graduate school!

CHAPTER 9

Using Humor Resources

There is always a laugh in the utterly familiar.

—JAMES THURBER, HUMORIST

THE PROCESS OF ENHANCING YOUR child's sense of humor should be fun for everyone. By now you are aware that this will be an ongoing project that does not have an obvious finish. You've learned the steps you can take to increase humor in your child's life—creating a humor-rich environment, planning humor-filled activities, and being on the lookout for humor-enriching opportunities that crop up unexpectedly. You're not alone in this worthy endeavor: there are humor resources you can turn to for ideas and laughs. Some humor resources can cost lots of money, but others are low in cost or even free! In fact, humor resources are everywhere and are limited only by the creative imaginations of you and your child.

WHAT ARE HUMOR RESOURCES?

Humor resources are those events, products, places, activities, and people that will help you build your child's sense of humor. They can include bookstores and libraries; the Internet; magic, novelty, and costume shops; toy stores; television and movie theaters; video and DVD rental stores; the circus, zoos, and parks; and maybe even your next door neighbor. While many of these resources may not be specifically humor related, fun activities and people do make it easier to create and spot humor. It may require some effort on your part (and your child's) to seek out the sometimes not-so-obvious humor in these resources. I'll try to help.

The biggest secret (until now) in locating humor resources is that they are *everywhere*—all around us every day in our interactions with people and in our observations of our environment. In fact, humor often comes from signs, labels, and newspaper headlines that were not intended to be funny. Take a look at these examples:

It takes a different mindset—one that imposes no restrictions whatsoever—to detect this type of humor. Parents can teach their children to become *joy trackers* or *humor spotters*—people who are sensitive to potential humor in everyday life, even when a humorous effect was not intended.

The section below discusses each resource and how you can tailor it to fit your objective of helping your child learn to appreciate and use humor. Although many of the following resources are designed to produce general enjoyment rather than hearty laughter, with a little ingenuity, you can use them to accomplish your goal.

Amusement Parks and Theme Parks (Expensive)

No doubt about it—these places *are* fun for the whole family. Unfortunately, they're also pricey. (If you're thinking about having a family vacation at one of these parks, be sure to check for special rates and discounts through your travel agent, on the Internet, or by calling the parks directly.) Amusement parks offer rides, games, and other forms of entertainment. A theme park— like Disneyland—is just an amusement park that's centered on one theme, in this case, Disney movies and cartoons. Many areas have a local amusement park, which is not as expensive as a nationally known theme park.

While amusement park rides may be thrilling and fun, they're not funny. So, in addition to enjoying the rides, be sure to interact with the costumed characters who often walk around the park. Some of these characters—Donald Duck, for instance— may already be familiar to your child. These individuals are there specifically to make your child smile and laugh.

Also, see the various scheduled shows at these parks, which often use humor to capture a child's attention. Enjoy the shows with your child. Laugh readily at the humor of the performers, as well as that of the animatronics attractions. And definitely visit the Fun House, which will usually have mirrors that distort your appearance. Some will make you look very tall or very wide or very small. It's funny to view your body in a way you've never seen it before.

What's very important here is that you *participate* in all these park activities with your child. Don't just stand around and *watch* your child have fun—be sure to have fun yourself! Your broad smile, laughter, and obvious pleasure will further encourage your child to let go and really enjoy all the attractions—and his time spent with you.

If these types of activities do not fit your budget, don't fret. Your child will certainly be able to learn humor skills without them.

Bookstores (Moderate Cost)

Are bookstores funny places? Not necessarily, but many of the books you will find there are. Some "super" bookstores are specifically designed to be child friendly. Not only do they have a large section just for children, they also have places where children can sit and peruse the books. While "super" bookstores are great resources, don't rule out smaller, independent bookstores, many of which sell children's books exclusively. Both types of stores are likely to have helpful employees who can assist you and your child in selecting humor-filled books. However, you may find that the salespeople at a children's bookstore are even more knowledgeable about what's available for kids.

When visiting a bookstore, be sure to ask the salesperson to name some of the more popular *funny* children's books. The clerk is sure to come up with quite a few. Once you and the salesperson help your child select several humor-filled books for his age level, allow him to look through the books to choose the funniest one to purchase. When you get the book home, be sure to read it with your child and talk about what's funny and why.

The books your child chooses don't necessarily have to be

joke or riddle books, of course, but they are great humor resources. There are countless examples of these types of books for young people. Two popular ones are *500 Hilarious Jokes for Kids* by Jeff Rovin and *1,000 Knock Knock Jokes for Kids* by Michael Kilgarriff. Of special interest are the samples of humor created *by kids* themselves and sent to comedian and TV host Rosie O'Donnell. She wrote the introduction to the collections in *Kids Are Punny: Jokes Sent by Kids to the Rosie O'Donnell Show* and *Kids Are Punny 2: More Jokes Sent by Kids to the Rosie O'Donnell Show*.

Joke and riddle books can be fun for kids to read and share, but in and of themselves, they may not do much to enhance the reader's own sense of humor. A good strategy is to go through some of the printed jokes and have your child "improve" those that he doesn't find funny. With older kids, the printed jokes can also be good starting points to write entirely new jokes about common themes, such as a talking car or a dog's attitude toward his so-called owner.

Poetry for children can also be very funny. For example, Jack Prelutsky's *New Kid on the Block* includes some hilarious poems. And let's not forget good old Dr. Seuss. His books always make young children laugh with their repetitive and nonsensical rhymes.

Do some research—check the Internet, read the children's book reviews in your newspaper, and ask your child's teacher. Find out what's funny in children's literature today, and direct your child to those books.

Carnivals and Fairs (Moderate Cost)

Carnivals and fairs can be lots of fun, but it can be a bit more difficult to find humor at these attractions than it is at amusement and theme parks. My advice to you is seek out the clown—there will usually be one hanging around. Also, look for face-painting booths. Your child can ask the artist to paint his face to look like a clown or something else that's silly. Be sure to take pictures for later laughs.

There may also be an artist who draws caricatures of people. These artists usually exaggerate a subject's prominent facial features, like big eyes or a big nose. When your child sees a caricature of himself, he'll surely laugh. (You, on the other hand, may walk away with such a picture of yourself wondering if your ears really *are* that big.)

A word of warning: The games at carnivals and fairs can often be very frustrating for kids (and for adults!). Winning any expensive prize is more difficult than hitting the state's lottery grand prize. You may want to steer clear of carnival games and save your bucks for the bookstore.

Children's Concerts (Moderate Cost)

The performers at concerts for children know that humor keeps kids interested, so the songs they sing and the stories they tell often have a humorous twist. By all means take your child to see some of the popular children's performers, such as Raffi, but don't disregard local entertainers. Check newspapers, the Internet, and your local community center for child-oriented concerts in your area, especially around holiday time. Many communities offer free concerts in the park throughout the year.

Circus (Moderate Cost)

Clown fans will claim that clowns are by far the funniest attraction you'll find at the circus. While everything else is going on—some of it not funny at all—there's always a clown in one of the rings to set your eyes upon. Your child may enjoy these entertainers' slapstick antics—from trying to squeeze into a small car to taunting the lion tamer to riding around in groups on mini bicycles. Remember, though, that some children do not like clowns. If your child is one of them, the circus probably isn't the best humor resource for him.

Internet (Low Cost)

The Internet is an incredible communication and information system. It can be an invaluable source of materials and activities that can help develop your child's sense of humor. Unfortunately, many adults are still not up to speed with this relatively new technology. If you're one of those people—and if you have a computer with Internet access—make it your business to learn as much as you can about surfing the web. To ease into it, read a book such as *Internet in an Hour for Beginners* by Don Mayo and Kathy Berkemeyer, or watch a video such as *The Internet for Beginners* by Alan Cummins, et al.

If you want to encourage your child to use the Internet as a humor resource, don't leave him to surf the web alone. Remember, a vital part of helping your child create and appreciate humor involves your active participation. Your guidance will be invaluable in locating and using humor resources on the web. Also, whether your child is using the Internet as a humor resource or not, you should always make it your business to monitor your child's Internet activities. See the inset "Monitoring Your Child's Internet Activities" on page 144, for some helpful tips.

Innumerable websites are devoted specifically to children. Most of these have humor-related information and activities for kids. But how do you find them? It's actually pretty easy. For starters, if you have the America Online Internet service, you will see that there is a "Kids Only" link that features children's books, products, and activities, some of which are humor oriented. As of now, this particular service has a game called "Comics by

Monitoring Your Child's Internet Activities

Like any powerful force, the Internet can be abused for a variety of negative, even criminal, purposes. In many cases, written laws have not caught up with skilled and innovative Internet abusers. The best defense for parents who wish to protect their children is to become comfortable with their computer and even more knowledgeable than their children about accessing the Internet.

To begin, consult the website http://www.rsac.org./ for guidance in determining which websites are suitable for your child. This is the site for the Internet Content Rating Association (ICRA), an independent, non-profit organization. Its aim is to protect children from potentially harmful material while continuing to protect the free-speech rights of content providers.

While you should spend time with your child at the computer, older children will undoubtedly want to spend time alone on the Internet. First, you will want to limit the amount of time your child actually spends at the computer. Why? Well, a child who is always at the computer isn't spending much time in the great outdoors, isn't getting much exercise, isn't socializing, and probably isn't developing his sense of humor. Second, you will want to make sure your child follows some basic rules:

1. Your child should *never* give out personal information to a website without your approval—this type of information can include his full name, his address, his date of birth, his parents' names, his telephone number, and so on. And never, never should he give out personal information to someone he meets in a chat room, including something as simple as his first name. (More about chat rooms below.) As far as e-mail is concerned, your child should keep all of his personal information out of his correspondence, no matter to whom he is writing.

2. If something your child sees on the Internet makes him uncomfortable, he should stop looking at it and let you know about it immediately. This goes for any e-mail that he may receive. If he receives an e-mail from someone he doesn't know, he should show it to you *before* it is opened. You can either delete it or read it and then deal with it accordingly.

3. Some children's websites require a password to access the games or maybe even the site itself. The password should be completely different from the password the family uses to log on to the Internet and should be hard for other people to guess; a combination of letters and numbers is best. Your child should share his passwords with you, but with nobody else.

4. Your child should be aware that all websites contain advertisements in the form of banners or links. He should always consult you before clicking on an advertisement. Some junk e-mail may also contain advertisements; it's best just to delete these without reading them.

5. You should decide whether or not your child may participate in *chats*—real-time discussions between people all over the world. Some chats are specifically for kids, but your child should be warned that not everyone who claims to be a kid really is a kid. There are some very disturbed people out there who may lure your child into a conversation. These people may offer gifts or may say any number of things, some of them funny, to get your child to confide in them. Be sure to warn your child about them the same way you would warn him about talking to strangers.

6. *Instant messaging* is a way that your child can communicate with his friends in a "private" window on the Internet. Chats between friends can often lead to humorous banter. You may hear your child *LOL*—a common chat abbreviation to let others know that you're *laughing out loud.* (Research has not yet determined what percentage of people who type LOL are actually laughing out loud at the time.)

If your child receives an instant message from someone he doesn't know, he shouldn't respond—if a website link is included in the instant message, he should not click on it. He should immediately alert you to any instant messages he receives from people he doesn't know. You can then handle it as you see fit.

If your child follows all of the above rules, the Internet can be a fun and safe place. For added precaution, some Internet services have parental control settings that allow you to create specific levels of access for your child's screen name, including Internet control access, use of instant messages, e-mail controls, chat controls, and so on. If your service provides such a feature, be sure to use it. It is wise to station the computer in a more public area, such as the family room, rather than the child's bedroom—even if no other family members use the computer. Like anything in life, the Internet can be put to good use or bad use. Make sure your child knows how to get the most out of it as you safeguard him from potential danger.

You," where kids can interact with a pre-drawn comic strip, without words or facial expressions. There are several different "faces"—happy, sad, mad, disgusted, surprised, and so on—that your child can drag and drop into the blank face areas. Your child can then go ahead and write captions for these comics. He can submit his creation to the comic gallery to be viewed later, and he can even view other comic strips created by kids.

To find specific websites for children's humor, use a *search engine.* A search engine is a website that searches through other websites on the Internet and provides you with links related to your search words. In this case, your search words could be *humor for kids* or *children's humor* or *children's humor websites*— or any variation. Note that if you just type in "humor," the links that the search engine provides will not necessarily be appropriate for children. So be careful in how you word your searches.

Some helpful search engines include www.about.com, www.altavista.com, www.askjeeves.com, www.dogpile.com, www.excite.com, www.hotbot.com, www.google.com, www.infoseek.com, www.iwon.com, www.lycos.com, www.netscape.com, and www.yahoo.com—the last of which also offers a link to the "Yahooligans" feature that contains topics of interest only to kids, some of it humor related. Many children's magazines have websites, as well. Use the name of the particular magazine your child is interested in as your search word. A link to that magazine's home page should be one of the first choices provided by the search engine. I can also recommend www.pbskids.org, an educational television site for kids, as an excellent humor resource.

The Internet is forever evolving and changing, so you will need to actively search the web for what's new in children's humor. Also visit your library and local bookstore, which are sure to have books that list the best websites for kids. (Also, see the Suggested Websites resource on page 169.)

It's important to note that many of the joke-a-day and humor sites are really intended for adults. As a parent, it is vital that you monitor a site before recommending it to your child. Also note that there are dozens of websites designed specifically for parents to provide guidance on various topics, such as television, movies, Internet use, and so on. Be creative with your search words to find these sites. Don't forget about using the Internet to search for children-specific events taking place in and around your area and to learn about amusement parks and other kid-friendly attractions.

The Internet can be a valuable resource that you can tap into and enjoy with your child as his sense of humor develops. Sit at the computer with him and go surfing without getting wet!

Kitchens (Low Cost)

A room with a television is fun, but a room with a refrigerator can be fun, too. Your kitchen has lots of humor potential. You don't play with your food? Well, why not? Food can be lots of fun, and you can even turn food-related activities into humor-filled activities. Different pasta shapes (uncooked) can be pasted on construction paper and painted to create funny-looking, noodle-nose characters. Kids can have contests for the best silly sundae or the funniest pizza design. Marshmallows and toothpicks can be used to make marshmallow people. (Different types of small candies can be used for the face and clothing.) The sillier looking the better. And what about making gingerbread people with funny faces and clothing? Carving a funny-faced pumpkin is a traditional Halloween kitchen activity.

Don't forget about the exercise in Chapter 5 which suggests that you use food coloring to create differently colored food, like green mashed potatoes and blue milk. Thanks to Heinz, just dipping a French fry in purple ketchup can create lots of laughs.

Remember to tailor food-related games to your child's maturity level, and, of course, to provide adult supervision in order to avoid food fights. The best part about this resource is that when you're all done, you can eat the results of the activity! That sure is cost-effective.

Libraries (Free!)

Be sure to check out your local library often. Like bookstores, libraries can be a great source for humor-filled books, but these books are free—that is, as long as they don't become overdue!

Ask the librarian to recommend funny books—he or she will be more than happy to help, and will probably come up with some books you may never have thought of on your own. Your child can pore over his finds at a child-sized desk or table while you visit the adult section. Libraries also have a section with the latest children's magazines, which you and your child can look through together. And don't forget the weekly story-reading sessions held by many libraries.

Most important, check with your library for information about local comedic shows and fun happenings for kids. Libraries often have this type of information available, and sometimes even post it on a bulletin board.

Live Theater (Moderate Cost)

Besides children's concerts, there are other live performances for children, including puppet shows, plays, and interactive musical theater groups. Some theater groups do adaptations of well-known children's stories, such a *Stuart Little* or *Alice in Wonderland*. While these examples aren't considered comedies, they do contain comic elements, as do most productions for children. These are the elements you will want to focus on with your child. Once again, check in newspapers, on the Internet, and with your local community center for live children's theater in your area.

Many communities have amateur theater activities that offer low-cost classes for people who are interested in increasing their acting skills. Ask your local theater group specifically about enrolling your nine- to twelve-year-old in improv classes. Improvisation allows your child to practice creating humor spontaneously. At the end of the session, you may even get to watch him in action.

Magazines and Newspapers (Low Cost)

Children's magazines can be excellent humor resources for parents searching for some new ideas to promote humor. You can flip through them for this purpose even when your child is not around. Keep in mind that not every article will be humor related, but some of the fictional stories and anecdotes will have a humorous twist. Also, kids' magazines usually have a joke and riddle page, poetry, and other humor-specific features. Children's magazines are also filled with fun games and activities that may be humor related, or that can be converted into something humor related.

There are so many magazines for children at every age level. A few that come to mind are *Babybug* (for children six months to two years old); *Sesame Street Magazine* (for kids ages two to five); *Nick, Jr.* (for preschoolers and parents); *Highlights* magazine (for kids from two to twelve); and *Nickelodeon Magazine* (for older preteen children). What's great about these magazines is that they include many activities and articles that tap into your child's other abilities and interests, in addition to the humor-oriented ones. As mentioned previously, many magazines also have websites. *Highlights,* for example, has its own website, www.highlightskids.com, a subscription-only site that offers no advertising. Its "Games and Giggles" section features the opportunity for children to read and create their own jokes and cartoons.

You can get your child a subscription to his favorite magazine, or you can buy a different one each month at your local bookstore or newsstand. As mentioned earlier, libraries also have magazines, which your child can look through at his leisure.

As for newspapers, they usually have a comics section that you and your child can read together. You can also use the comic strips for the "Create a Caption" exercise discussed in Chapter 5.

(See page 75.) Some Sunday editions have a section just for kids, such as *Kidsday*. But that's not all that newspapers are good for. They also have movie listings, book reviews, and information about local happenings—information that can alert you to great humor resources.

Magic Stores, Novelty Shops, and Costume Shops (Moderate Cost)

These types of stores are comedy mines for kids. Admittedly, not every town has one of these stores, but if you do some research, including checking the yellow pages, you can probably find one within driving distance. What will your child find there? Funny wigs, rubber noses, costumes, gadgets, balloons, face paints, putty, cans of "slime," crayons, oversized shoes, colorful T-shirts with funny sayings on them, and more. These humor props and tools are relatively inexpensive. But watch out, they can add up! As your child browses the store, discuss how those items can be used at home to create humor.

Be sure to ask the salesclerk if he knows of any humor-related activities going on in the store or in the neighborhood. Often, the people who frequent these stores are performers of some kind, so the salesclerk may have some inside information.

Movie Theaters (Moderate Cost)

Check your local movie listings for theaters near you that are currently showing movies for kids. New movies are coming out all the time. Be sure that you read the reviews of movies before you go see them, though. Some movies may seem as if they were made for children, when in actuality the humor in them is hostile or obscene—such as in the *South Park* movies. Most movies for children aren't advertised as comedies, of course, but they generally contain comical elements, which you can enjoy along with your child and talk about later.

Pay attention to the movie ratings. G-rated movies are appropriate for all young children. These are the movies you may want to seek out most often. A movie with a PG rating may contain material that is unsuitable for children. Reading reviews about a movie with a PG rating may help you decide if it is, in fact, suitable for your child. The PG-13 rating strongly cautions parents that some material may be inappropriate for children under thirteen. You may want to avoid these movies entirely until your child reaches his teen years. Movies rated R and NC-17 are best avoided by children altogether. The questionable material in movies rated PG and up is usually sexual, violent, or obscene in nature, to varying degrees.

Parks and Beaches (Free!)

Parks and beaches in themselves are not funny places, but if you keep your eyes open and your humor-spotting detector on, you may witness a lot of funny happenings. The best part about going to these places is that it gives you a chance to spend time with your child outdoors, during which you can share jokes, riddles, and funny stories. If you do see something humorous, be sure to point it out and, once you're finished laughing, talk about why it was funny. Some parks and beaches have miniature golf courses designed around entertaining themes that may produce some laughs while you play.

Party Planners (Moderate Cost)

Parties can be great opportunities for humor. But simply having children over to eat cake doesn't guarantee fun or laughs. For a relatively small fee per child, party-planning companies will produce an entire special event around a funny theme of your child's choice—the circus or a favorite cartoon show, for example. The professional planner does all the work and is an expert at making the party fun for all the young guests. If you don't want to pay the fee, be your own party planner. It's easy. Just check out a few of the many books that are available on planning a party for kids. Ask your local librarian or a salesperson at a bookstore to recommend one. (Also, see the Suggested Readings on page 167.)

There are a lot of fun things you can come up with on your own, too. For example, instead of giving the kids plain old party hats to wear, attach several balloons to each one. The kids can even make their own funny party hats as an activity. Also, many of the humor-creation exercises mentioned in Chapter 5 can be converted into party activities. And, if you know a professional clown or a funny magician, hire him to come over for a half hour or so to entertain the kids.

It doesn't matter whether your party is elaborate or simple; kids who participate in humor-filled activities will be "kids who laugh."

People (Free!)

We all know people who always seem to be laughing and are just plain fun to be around. Not only do funny people say funny things, but funny things happen to them, too. Actually, the very same things happen to everyone else, but these people can extract the humor in those everyday events and share it with others. We also know people who are just the opposite—they have the uncanny ability to detect the tarnish in every silver lining. Kids readily tune into these differences in attitude and quickly mimic any adults around them. Therefore, it's a good idea to expose your child to as many cheerful, optimistic, positive, smiling, and *funny* people as possible.

When you use people as humor resources, they don't have to

be constantly telling memorized jokes or creating balloon wiener dogs or wearing pink wigs. To do so occasionally might be fun, but we mostly want these key people to be *ready* to laugh at any time and to *try* to create humor frequently.

Street Performances for Kids (Free!)

If you live in or near a city that has street performances—or if you are visiting one—seek out these shows with your child. Some of these performances may even be advertised in local papers. If you're lucky, you may pass by a street performance on your way to someplace else. Be sure to stop and watch.

Street performances usually take place in large public areas, such as Nathaniel Hall in Boston, Inner Harbor in Baltimore, Balboa Park in San Diego, and Ghiardelli's Square in San Francisco. These performances enhance the character of a city, so cities often issue permits to entertainers like mimes, jugglers, magicians, puppeteers, and musicians to perform in designated areas. Some of these performers are actually paid by the city; others may have a bucket handy for your contributions. Tossing in a few coins will provide these artists with financial humor support.

While it's true that not all of these performances will be humor related or will be for kids, it's worthwhile to stop and watch. If you and your child get some laughs out of it, all the better.

Toy Stores (Moderate Cost to Expensive)

When was the last time you lost yourself in a toy store? Kids do it all the time. There's so much to see, and if it's one of those stores that are designed so kids can play with the display models, there's so much to try. But are toys humor resources? It depends on which toys and on how your child plays with them. Dressing dolls and knocking down action figures may be fun activities for children, but they are not directly humor promoting. On the other hand, if your child makes the dolls or action figures do and say funny things, they can actually be used for humor-creation practice. Some toys, such as Tickle Me Elmo, are designed specifically to be humorous—they either look funny or may "say" and do funny things, if they're battery operated. There are even laughter machines that produce recorded laughter at the touch of a button. These types of toys are fine in moderation for humor-appreciation practice.

Don't make the mistake of relying on the most technologically advanced toys and computer games to occupy your child's time. We all know of at least one young child who received an expensive gift of some battery-operated toy, but ended up spending most of the time playing with the box it came in because it allowed his imagination to carry him to unknown frontiers of fun.

Video and DVD Rental Stores (Low Cost)

Your local video/DVD rental store should have a section just for kids and family entertainment. Often, the people who work there can help you pick out comedies suited for kids. I'd like to recommend the movie *The Great Race*, which features one of the best pie fights ever recorded. The Muppet movies are also always a big hit with kids. You may want to look at a movie guide, such as *The Movie Mom's Guide to Family Movies* by Nell Minow, to help you decide what to rent. Remember to watch the movie with your child, and don't forget about the exercise in Chapter 5 that suggests stopping the movie at key points to discuss what humorous event might happen next.

The Zoo (Moderate Cost)

Animals are funny to us humans! They may not intend to be funny, but they do funny things nonetheless. Monkeys are probably the funniest animals you'll come across at the zoo. Just watch their antics for a little while and you're sure to start smiling and laughing. And who knows how funny the monkeys think we are? In Chapter 5, one of the activities suggests that you imitate the moneys. (See page 82.) If you do, remember to take pictures so that you can get even more laughs later on.

CRITERIA FOR JUDGING HUMOR RESOURCES

You are in the best position to evaluate potential humor resources for you and your child. When considering whether an item or experience would be a valuable humor resource, try to answer several important questions. Is the resource humor related? Is it appropriate for your child's age? Can you afford it? Are there any hidden agendas? Does it give you a chance to spend time with your child? Each of these considerations will be discussed below so that you can start taking advantage of available humor resources in the wisest way possible.

Is It Humor Related?

When evaluating humor resources, be critical, and try to judge whether a given game or activity is humor related. Video and computer games, for instance, may be described as "fun," and certainly can eat up your child's time, but they are unlikely to help develop his sense of humor. In fact, in many cases, they can turn your child into a humorless zombie.

It is important to make the subtle distinction between "fun" and "funny." Certainly, you want to encourage your child to have fun playing games and reading books, but your primary interest in this book is to help develop your child's sense of humor. So while your child may enjoy doing things that aren't humor related—and while there's certainly nothing wrong with that—you want to make sure that many of his activities, toys, and experiences are, in fact, going to directly facilitate his appreciation and creation of humor.

Is It Age Appropriate?

Often, the age range printed on children's games and toys is very broad. Clearly, different humor materials are suitable for children of different ages. Take another look at the humor-creation exercises recommended in Chapter 5. They are arranged by age so that young children will not become frustrated by being asked to try something that is too difficult, and older children will not become bored with an activity designed for younger children. When considering which humor resources to use and how to use them, keep your child's maturity level in mind. For example, some children's books and stories can be quite scary to children once they learn the meanings of the words. The lullaby "Rock-a-Bye Baby" has a disastrous outcome—*and down will come baby, cradle and all!* Falling from the treetops is not fun or recommended. The wolf's huffing and puffing and blowing the house down in *The Three Little Pigs* is not comforting to a child who should feel that his home is a safe haven. Generally, reading such nursery rhymes to your preverbal child will be totally harmless. For children who understand the words you read, though, try something a little lighter.

Is It Affordable?

Can you afford a given humor resource and, if so, is it worth the money? If you choose to pay the considerable costs to attend any of the major theme parks for some special occasion, it should be a great experience for you and your child. However, such expenses are certainly not necessary in the process of increasing your child's sense of humor. A trip to the beach or a walk in the mountains can be both fun and free. You can tell jokes or share humorous stories along the way. And what about the costs of toys, books, humor props, concerts, and so on? It is reasonable to pay a fair price for these products. Certainly, these aren't as expensive as a trip to a theme park, but you will nevertheless want to consider their potential to increase your child's sense of humor before making a purchase.

Is There a Hidden Agenda?

It's important for you to determine whether or not a book, web-site, or toy, for example, has some other underlying agenda. Some resources are merely commercial gimmicks designed to make high-priced sales or to add your name to a mailing list. Others promote a specific religious point of view. Pay close attention to this issue to determine whether your child will be influenced by the potential humor resource to buy more products or to adopt new religious beliefs.

Does It Promote Time Spent Together?

Watching a funny movie with your child is fine, but it is only half the fun. It's just as important to take the time to talk to your child about what he thinks or likes about the movie. This advice applies to reading with your child and participating in any of the recommended humor-related activities. So, when considering a humor resource, think about whether it will allow you to spend time with your child to discuss the humorous aspects of the resource. Sure, your child can enjoy time alone or with friends doing humorous things, but be sure that many of the humor resources you use enable you to be present—not only to provide humor feedback but also to share the fun.

CONCLUSION

In this chapter, we encourage you to consider all of the humor resources available to you. The best resources allow room for your child's sense of humor to grow. A young child may laugh at a particular event or story, but as he develops and changes, he will find humor in increasingly subtle and sophisticated sources, marking his progress toward adolescence and adulthood.

Remember, however, that humor resources are only half the story. Sure, they may get your child to laugh, but when you *share* the laughter with your child—watching a funny movie together, browsing the magic shop, enjoying a street performance, and so on—your child sees you laugh, and the concept of humor becomes more compelling in his own life. One of the best ways to experience unforgettable personal closeness with your child is to share humor and warm laughter.

Don't forget that the extent of potential humor stimuli in your daily environment is truly unlimited—and, of course, your own humorous perceptions and observations are totally free! It's most important to set a good humor-making example in your own behavior and to guide your child in spotting humor wherever he goes.

Conclusion

ARE YOU ARE READY TO START ENHANCING your child's sense of humor—to provide the guidance, structure, and support needed for this worthy endeavor? Sure you are. Like most parents, you want your child to be well adjusted socially and well liked by her peers. Kids who laugh are treasures to others—their parents, their siblings, their teachers, and their circle of friends. In fact, a keen sense of humor may be one of the most important and lasting gifts you can give to your child.

You've learned about the many advantages that a humorous outlook can provide for your child, including creative thinking, self-confidence, optimism, and the ability to cope with bullies and make new friends. You've also learned about the importance of becoming sensitized to the many humor stimuli in this crazy world—including things that were not originally intended to be comical. This is a major skill for all humor appreciators, parents and kids alike.

There will be lots of opportunities for your child to exercise her sense of humor and reap its many benefits. If you follow the recommendations in this book, and even add some creative ideas of your own, your child will be very lucky and happy indeed. Your mind is probably buzzing with great ideas, and you're probably itching to put this book down and get started. It'll still be here when you want to refer to it. So go ahead—scratch that itch and get them laughing!

References

Bernstein, Deena K. "The development of humor: Implications for assessment and intervention," *Topics in Language Disorders* 6 (4) (1986): 65–71.

Cart, Michael. *What's So Funny? Wit and Humor in American Children's Literature.* New York: Harper Collins, 1995.

Cherkas, Lynn, Fran Hochberg, Alex J. MacGregor, Harold Snieder, and Tim D. Spector. "Happy families: A twin study of humour," *Twin Research* 33 (2000): 17–22.

Cornett, Claudia E. *Learning Through Laughter: Humor in the Classroom.* Bloomington, IN: Phi Delta Kappa Educational Foundation, 1986.

Durant, John, and Jonathan Miller, editors. *Laughing Matters: A Serious Look at Humour.* Essex, England: Longman Scientific & Technical, 1988.

Ellison, Sheila, and Barbara Ann Barnett. *365 Ways to Raise Great Kids.* Naperville, IL: Sourcebooks, 1998.

Gruner, Charles R. *The Game of Humor: A Comprehensive Theory of Why We Laugh.* New Brunswick, NJ: Transaction Publishers, 1997.

————. *Understanding Laughter: The Workings of Wit & Humor.* Chicago: Nelson-Hall, 1978.

Hay, Jennifer. "The pragmatics of humor support," *Humor: International Journal of Humor Research* 14 (2001): 55–82.

Hunsaker, Johanna S. "It's no joke: Using humor in the classroom," *Clearing House* 61 (1988): 285–286.

Kappas, Katharine H. "A developmental analysis of children's responses to humor," *The Literary Quarterly* 37, No. 1 (1967): 67–77.

Kataria, Madan. *Laugh for No Reason.* Mumbai, India: Madhuri International, 1999.

Lefcourt, Herbert M. *Humor: The Psychology of Living Buoyantly.* New York: Kluwer Academic/Plenum Publishers, 2001.

MacHovec, Frank J. *Humor: Theory, History, Applications.* Springfield, IL: Charles C. Thomas, 1988.

Martin, Rod A. "Humor, laughter, and physical health: Methodological issues and research findings," *Psychological Bulletin* 127 (2001): 504–519.

McGee, Paul E. *How to Develop Your Sense of Humor.* Dubuque, IA: Kendall/Hunt Publishing Co., 1994.

————. *Humor: Its Origin and Development.* San Francisco: W.H. Freeman and Co., 1979.

McGhee, Paul E., and A.J. Chapman, editors. *Children's Humour.* New York: John Wiley and Sons, 1980.

Mindess, Harvey. "The sense in humor," *Saturday Review* (August 21, 1971): 10–12.

Morreall, John, editor. *The Philosophy of Laughter and Humor.* Albany: State University of New York Press, 1987.

Newman, Dawn A., Arthur M. Horne, and Christi L. Bartolomucci. *Bully Busters: A Teacher's Manual.* Champaign, IL: Research Press, 2000.

Nilsen, Alleen Pace, and Don L.F. Nilsen. *Encyclopedia of 20th-Century American Humor.* Phoenix: Oryx Press, 2000.

Provine, Robert R. *Laughter: A Scientific Investigation.* New York: Viking/Penguin Putnam, Inc., 2000.

Rogers, Vincent R. "Laughing with children," *Educational Leadership* 42 (1984): 46–50.

Ruch, Willibald, and Franz-Josef Hehl. "A two-mode model of humor appreciation: Its relation to aesthetic appreciation and simplicity-complexity of personality," in *The Sense of Humor: Explorations of a Personality Characteristic.* New York: Mouton de Gruyter, 1998: 109–142.

Schroeder, Beverly Allred. *Human Growth and Development.* Saint Paul, MN: West Publishing Company, 1992.

Simon, Neil. *Neil Simon Rewrites: A Memoir.* New York: Simon and Schuster, 1996.

Whitt, J. Kenneth, and Norman M. Prentice. "Cognitive processes in the development of children's enjoyment and comprehension of joking riddles," *Developmental Psychology* 13 (1977): 129–136.

Suggested Readings

Clever Party Planning by Suzanne Singleton (Twenty-Nine Angels Publishing, 1999).

Consumer Guide, 101 Best Web Sites for Kids by Trevor Meers (New American Library, 1999).

Disney A to Z: The Official Encyclopedia by Dave Smith (Hyperion, 1996).

51 Best Ways to Amuse Kids by Ellen Van Wees (Berkley Publishing Group/Penguin Putnam, 2000).

500 Hilarious Jokes for Kids by Jeff Rovin (New American Library, 1990).

Humor, Play & Laughter: Stress-Proofing Life With Your Kids by Joseph A. Michelli (Love and Logic Press, 1998).

Kids Are Punny: Jokes Sent by Kids to the Rosie O'Donnell Show by Rosie O'Donnell (Warner Books, 1997).

Kids Are Punny 2: More Jokes Sent by Kids to the Rosie O'Donnell Show by Rosie O'Donnell (Warner Books, 1998).

Kids' Party Games and Activities by Penny Warner (Meadowbrook Press, 1993).

The Laughing Classroom: Everyone's Guide to Teaching With Humor and Play by Diane Loomans and Karen Kolberg (New World Library, 1993).

Laughing Lessons: 149 $^{2}/_{3}$ Ways to Make Teaching and Learning Fun by Ron Burgess (Free Spirit Publishing, 2000).

More Films Kids Like: A Catalog of Short Films for Children by Maureen Gaffney (American Library Association, 1977).

The Movie Mom's Guide to Family Movies by Nell Minow (Avon Books, 1999).

1,000 Knock Knock Jokes for Kids by Michael Kilgarriff (Ballantine Books, 1990).

What to Do When the Lights Go On: A Comprehensive Guide to 16mm Films and Related Activities for Children by Maureen Gaffney and Gerry Bond Laybourne (Oryx Press, 1981).

Suggested Websites

Halife

Website: www.halife.com/kids/kids.html

This sites includes jokes, riddles, and other fun activities for kids, as well as humor for adults that is nonetheless appropriate for family consumption.

Highlights for Children

Website: www.highlightskids.com

A subscription-only site, Highlights for Children offers a range of games and stories, including a "Games and Giggles" section.

Humor Matters

Website: www.humormatters.com/kidsjoke

Part of a larger site "dedicated to the power and practice of positive therapeutic humor," this site presents a slew of kid-safe riddles.

The Humor Project, Inc.

Website: www.humorproject.com

Created by the first organization in the world to focus full-time on the positive power of humor, this site offers articles, interviews, book suggestions, and other humor-related information.

Kidsjokes

Website: www.kidsjokes.co.uk/

Although this British site features British spellings, it presents universal humor in the form of thousands of kids jokes arranged by category—doctor jokes, knock-knock jokes, silly jokes, and much more.

#1 All Kids Humor

Website: http://kidhumor.glowport.com

This website offers "family-safe fun," including a wealth of jokes in a variety of categories, from animal humor to school humor.

PBS Kids

Website: www.pbskids.org

Created by the Public Broadcasting Service, PBS Kids provides a joke site, games, silly stories, and many more fun—and funny—activities for kids.

Squigly's Playhouse

Website: www.squiglysplayhouse.com

Squigly's Playhouse presents jokes and riddles sent in by children around the world, as well as puzzles, brain teasers, and more.

Yahooligans!

Website: www.yahooligans.com

Billed as "the web guide for kids," this site leads kids to numerous activities and resources, including jokes and riddles.

Index

A

Abbott and Costello, 44, 131
Absurdity, 22
Acting Out exercise, 73
Activities, humor-related. *See*
    Classroom exercises; Exercises,
    humor-creation.
Adams, Hunter "Patch," 115
Add-Ons exercise, 71
Adulthood, 56
Age, conceptual. *See* Conceptual age.
Age/development considerations
    for humor creation, 67–68
    for humor resources, 157
    See also Humor, preferences and
    development, stages of.
Aggressive humor. *See* Hostile
    humor.
Allen, Steve, 65, 118
Allen, Woody, 94
America Online Internet service, 143
Amusement parks, as a humor
    resource, 139–140

Animals, play and, 39–40
Aniston, Jennifer, 118
Appreciation of humor, 10
    barriers to, 53, 55–56
    learning, 53
    media's effect on, 55
    other children's effect on, 54
    parents' effect on, 54
    siblings' effect on, 54
    society's effect on, 56–57
    strategy for developing, 52–53
April Fools' Day exercise, 128
April Fools' Day jokes. *See* Practical
    jokes.
Arthur, 34
Assertiveness, promoting, 57–58
Associative play, 38
Autism, humor studies in, 105–107

B

Babybug magazine, 150
Backward Dinner exercise, 75
Balboa Park, 154

Ball, Lucille, 44
Barnett, Barbara Ann, 65
Barney, 34
Bathroom humor, 93–94
Beaches, as a humor resource, 152
Berkemeyer, Kathy, 143
Between the Lions, 34
Bippus, Amy M., 85
Body dysmorphic disorder, 91
Bookstores, as a humor resource,
    140–141
Brainstorming, 75, 128
Brainstorming Games exercise,
    128–129
Bumper Stickers exercise, 131
Bunyan, Paul, 22
Byars, Betsy, 21

C

Callahan, John, 111
Caricatures, 142
Carnivals, as a humor resource,
    141–142
Cart, Michael, 32, 65, 98
Cartoons, 34
Cartoons and Captions exercise,
    77–78. *See also* Create a Caption
    exercise.
Chaplin, Charlie, 24, 131
Chats, Internet, 145
Cherkas, Lynn, 6
Children with special needs. *See*
    Special needs children.
Children's, other, effect on humor
    appreciation, 54
Children's concerts, as a humor
    resource, 142
Children's humor, categories of. *See*
    Humor, children's, categories of.

Circus, as a humor resource,
    142–143
Class clown competition, 121
Class clowns, dealing with, 118–120
Classroom, humor in the, 117–135
Classroom exercises
    April Fools' Day, 128
    Brainstorming Games, 128–129
    Bumper Stickers, 131
    Clay, 124
    Daffynitions, 131
    Daily Humor Sharing, 129
    Exaggerations, 129
    for fifth and sixth grades,
        131–134
    for first and second grades,
        125–128
    Friday Fun Time, 125–126
    Funny Costumes, 124
    Humor Diary, 131–132
    Humor Lesson, 132
    Humor Surveys, 132
    Humor Text, 129
    Humor-Creativity Game, 126
    Humor-Filled Classroom
        Environment, 126
    Humorous Speech Contest, 132
    Humorous Speechmaking
        Behaviors, 129
    Laughs on Command, 126–127
    Outlaw Humor, 130
    Photo Captions, 130
    Pictures, 124–125
    Pre-Halloween Day, 124
    for preschool and kindergarten,
        124–125
    Real Clown in Class, 127
    Report on a Comedian, 132
    Report on a Comedy, 133

School Jokes Catalog, 133
Share Your Blunders Game, 130
Show and Tell, 125
Sounds and Words, 130
Spoonerisms and Oxymorons, 133–134
Story Time, 125
Surprise the Kids, 125
Telephone Game, 127–128
for third and fourth grades, 128–131
Tom Swifties, 134
Watch a Comedy Classic, 130–131
See also Exercises, humor-creation.
Clay exercise, 124
Clown club, 134–135
Clowns, 142. *See also* Class clown competition; Class clowns, dealing with.
Comebacks, 112
Comedy Show exercise, 78
Comprehension of humor, 9–10
Conceptual age, 42
Conceptual incongruities, 28
Concerts, children's. *See* Children's concerts, as a humor resource.
Conundrum, 25
Cooperative play, 38
Cornett, Claudia, 123
Costume shops. *See* Magic stores, novelty shops, and costume shops, as a humor resource.
Crazy Animal Sounds exercise, 71, 73
Create a Caption exercise, 75. *See also* Cartoons and Captions exercise.
Creation of humor. *See* Humor creation.
Cummins, Alan, 143

D

Daffynitions exercise, 131
Daily Humor Sharing exercise, 129
Defenseless humor, 110–111
practicing, 112
Defiance, 22
Dinnertime, using humor during, 67
"Dirty" words, 93–94
Disneyland, 139
Dr. Seuss. *See* Geisel, Theodore.
Doctors office, spotting humor at, 113–115
Down syndrome, humor studies in, 105–107
Dragon Tales, 34

E

Ellison, Sheila, 65
Ellsworth, J'Anne, 103
Empathy, promoting, 98–99
Encyclopedia of 20th-Century American Humor (Nilsen), 34
Endogenous smiling, 42
Endorphins, 44
Everyday humor, 66–67
Exaggeration, 22
Exaggerations exercise, 129
Exercises, humor-creation
Acting Out, 73
Add-Ons, 71
for ages nine to twelve, 77–81
for ages one to three, 71, 73
for ages six to nine, 75–77
for ages three to six, 73–74
for ages three to twelve, 81–82
Backward Dinner, 75
Cartoons and Captions, 77–78
Comedy Show, 78

Crazy Animal Sounds, 71
Create a Caption, 75
Funny Faces, 69
Funny Home Videos, 81
Funny Stories, 75–76
Funny Uses, 76
Greeting Card Humor, 78
Ha, Ha!, 76
Halloween in July, 78
Humor Props, 81–82
Make Me Laugh, 82
Mimic Animal Behavior, 73–74
Monkey See, Monkey Do, 82
for newborns to age one, 69–71
Out-of-Season Holiday Songs, 79
Peek-a-Boo Game, 69
Physical Stimulation, 70
Puns, 79
Reverse Order, 79
Rhymes, 74
Rhyming Names, 73
Riddles, 77
Silly Sounds, 70
Sing Songs, 71
skills for, 67–68
Staring Contest, 74
Strange Colors, 74
Tongue Twisters, 79–80
What Happens Next?, 80
What's Funny About Not-So-
    Funny Things?, 81
Word Play, 77
See also Classroom exercises.
Exogenous smiling, 42
Expression of humor, 10

F

Fairs, as a humor resource, 141–142

False smiling. *See* Endogenous
    smiling.
Fantasy play, 39
Far Side, The, 6, 7
Feedback on negative humor, 96–98.
    See also Humor support.
500 Hilarious Jokes for Kids (Rovin),
    141
Five senses, the, 8
Flexibility, 11
Food, playing with. *See* Kitchens, as
    a humor resource.
Fox, Michael J., 110
Freud, Sigmund, 15, 16, 17
Friday Fun Time exercise, 125–126
Funny Costumes exercise, 124
Funny Faces exercise, 69
Funny Home Videos exercise, 81
Funny Stories exercise, 75–76
Funny Uses exercise, 76

G

Games, humor-related. *See*
    Classroom exercises; Exercises,
    humor-creation.
Geisel, Theodore, 46
Gender differences, 17–18
    preschoolers and, 28
    preteens and, 31
Gesell, Izzy, 37
Ghiardelli's Square, 154
Grandma's Rule, 66
Great Race, The, 155
Greeting Card Humor exercise, 78
Gruner, Charles, 16–17, 43

H

Ha, Ha! exercise, 76

Halloween in July exercise, 78
Hanly, Sheila, 33
Hartley, David, 51
Hay, Jennifer, 63
Hehl, Franz-Josef, 9, 10
Heinz, 148
Henderson, Rickey, 81
Highlights magazine, 150
"Ho Ho Ha Ha" game, 127
Holiday Songs exercise, Out-of-
    Season, 79
Horseplay, physical. *See* Slapstick.
Hospitals. *See* Doctors office,
    spotting humor at.
Hostile humor, 88, 90
Human Genome Project, 95
Human predicaments, 23
Humility, 13–14
Humor
    abusive, 85–86
    appreciation of, 10, 52–53
    attempts, when not to make, 86
    bathroom, 93–94
    children's, categories of, 22–26
    classroom, in the, 117–135
    comprehension of, 9–10
    as a coping device, 108–112
    creation of. *See* Humor creation.
    defenseless, 110–112
    defined, 8
    determining if something is
        related to, 156–157
    development. *See* Humor,
        preferences and development,
        stages of.
    at the doctor's office, 113–115
    effects of, 99–100
    everyday, 66–67
    expression of, 10
    feedback on attempts at. *See*
        Humor, negative, feedback on;
        Humor support.
    forms of, 12
    hostile, 88, 90
    hurtful versus healthy, 87–88
    inappropriate, 88, 89, 90–96
    incorporating, in the classroom,
        120–123
    in literature, 32
    in movies, 35–36
    modeling, 52, 58–60
    negative, feedback on, 96–98
    play and, 39
    preferences and development,
        stages of, 26–31
    resources. *See* Humor resources.
    self-effacing, 109–110, 112
    shaping, 52–53, 61–64
    special needs children and,
        103–115
    stereotypically based, 94–95
    strategy for developing
        appreciation of, 52–53
    subjects and expressions of, 12
    support, 53, 61–64
    on television, 32–35
    theories of, 14–17
    verbal, 24–26
    violent, 26
    See also Sense of humor.
Humor, Play & Laugher (Michelli), 108
Humor Center, the, 80
Humor creation, 10
    encouraging, 65–69
    See also Classroom exercises;
        Exercises, humor-creation.
Humor dates, 47

Humor Diary exercise, 131–132
Humor Lesson exercise, 132
Humor preferences
  of babies, 27–28
  of children ages eight to ten, 30
  of children ages eleven to twelve,
    30–31
  of children ages five to seven,
    29–30
  of children ages thirteen and up,
    31
  of preschoolers, 28–29
  of toddlers, 27–28
Humor Props exercise, 81–82
Humor resources, 137–138
  age-appropriateness of,
    determining, 157
  amusement parks, 139–140
  bookstores, 140–141
  carnivals, 141–142
  children's concerts, 142
  circus, 142–143
  cost considerations of, 157–158
  criteria for judging, 156–158
  hidden agendas in, 158
  Internet, 143, 146–148
  kitchens, 148
  libraries, 148–149
  live theater, 149
  magazines and newspapers,
    150–151
  magic stores, novelty shops, and
    costume shops, 151
  movie theaters, 151–152
  parks and beaches, 152
  party planners, 152–153
  people, 153–154
  street performances, 154
  theme parks, 139–140
  toy stores, 154–155
  what they are, 137–138
  zoo, 155–156
Humor spotters, 138–139
Humor support, 53, 61–64
  components of, 63
  See also Feedback on negative
    humor.
Humor Surveys exercise, 132
Humor Test exercise, 129
Humor-Creativity Game exercise,
  126
Humor-Filled Classroom
  Environment exercise, 126
Humorous perspective, qualities of,
  11, 13–14
Humorous Speech Contest exercise,
  132
Humorous Speechmaking
  Behaviors exercise, 129
Humor-related behavior
  modeling, 52
  shaping, 52–53

I

ICRA. *See* Internet Content Rating
  Association.
Improvisation, 149
Incongruity, 23
  conceptual, 28
  in the environment, 27–28
  unresolved, 25
Incongruity theory of humor, the, 16
Inner Harbor, 154
Instant messaging, 145–146
Intellectual play, 39
Internet, the
  as a humor resource, 143,
    146–148

monitoring your child's activity on, 144–146

Internet Content Rating Association (ICRA), 144

Internet for Beginners, The (Cummins), 143

Internet in an Hour for Beginners (Mayo and Berkemeyer), 143

J

James, Clive, 5

Jesting, 17

Jewell, Gerri, 110

Joke façade, 17

Jokes, 24
  bathroom-related. *See* Bathroom humor.
  practical. *See* Practical jokes.

Joking, stages of development, 17

Joy trackers, 138–139

K

Kataria, Madan, 50

Keaton, Buster, 24

Kidding, 96

Kids', other, effect on humor appreciation. *See* Children's, other, effect on humor appreciation.

Kids Are Punny: Jokes Sent by Kids to the Rosie O'Donnell Show (O'Donnell), 141

Kids Are Punny 2: More Jokes Sent by Kids to the Rosie O'Donnell Show (O'Donnell), 141

Kidsday, 151

Kilgarriff, Michael, 141

Kitchens, as a humor resource, 148

L

Lane, Nathan, 110

Larson, Gary, 6

Laughing parent, the, 49

Laughs on Command exercise, 126–127

Laughter, 27, 41–46
  in adults, 50
  in babies, 42–43
  biological benefits of, 44–46
  increasing, in children, 47–49
  not associated with humor, 46
  social contagion principle of, 118

Laughter clubs movement, 50

Laurel and Hardy, 131

Learning Through Laughter: Humor in the Classroom (Cornett), 123

Lefcourt, Herbert, 45

Lewis, Richard, 118

Libraries, as a humor resource, 148–149

Literature, children's, 32

Live theater, as a humor resource, 149

M

MacHovec, Frank, 99, 100

Magazines, as a humor resource, 150

Magic stores, novelty shops, and costume shops, as a humor resource, 151

Make Me Laugh exercise, 82

Marx Brothers, the, 44, 131

Mayo, Don, 143

Media, effect of, on humor appreciation, 55

Melbourne International Comedy Festival, 121
Michelli, Joseph A., 108
Miller, Dennis, 118
Mimic Animal Behavior exercise, 73–74
Mindess, Harvey, 11, 14, 122
Minow, Nell, 155
Mr. Rogers' Neighborhood, 34
Mockery, 23
Modeling humor, 52, 58–60
   during negative events, 59–60
Monkey See, Monkey Do exercise, 82
Monsters, Inc., 131
Moore, Dudley, 110
Morreall, John, 16
Movie Mom's Guide to Family Movies, The (Minow), 155
Movie ratings, 152
Movie theaters, as a humor resource, 151–152
Movies, children's, 35–36
Murdock Elementary School, 134

N

Nathaniel Hall, 154
National Institutes of Health, 95
Nature versus nurture debate, 6–8
New Kid on the Block (Prelutsky), 141
Newspapers, as a humor resource, 150
Nick, Jr. magazine, 150
Nickelodeon Magazine, 150
Nickelodeon network, 35, 111
Nilsen, Alleen, 34
Nilsen, Don, 34
Nonsense. *See* Rhyming and nonsense.

Nonsocial play, 38
Northwestern University, 63
Novelty shops. *See* Magic stores, novelty shops, and costume shops, as a humor resource.
Nurture versus nature debate, 6–8

O

O'Donnell, Rosie, 141
1,000 Knock Knock Jokes for Kids (Kilgarriff), 141
Outlaw Humor exercise, 130
Out-of-Season Holiday Songs exercise, 79
Oxymorons. *See* Spoonerisms and Oxymorons exercise.

P

Parallel play, 38
Parent, the laughing, 49
Parents
   of class clowns, 120
   effect of, on humor appreciation, 54
   effect of, on personality, 8
   expectations of, for special needs children, 107–108
Parks, as a humor resource, 152. *See also* Amusement parks, as a humor resource; Theme parks, as a humor resource.
Party planners, as a humor resource, 152–153
Patch Adams, 115
PBS. *See* Public Broadcasting Service.
Peek-A-Boo! 100 Ways to Make a Baby Smile (Hanly), 33
Peek-a-boo game, 24, 27, 33

Peek-a-Boo Game exercise, 69–70
Pelswick, 111
People, as a humor resource, 153–154
Performances, street. *See* Street performances.
Personal targets, 90–91
Personality, parents' effect on, 8
Phony phone calls, 93
Photo Captions exercise, 130
Physical Stimulation exercise, 70
Physical stimuli, 27, 46, 70
Physically disabled children. *See* Special needs children.
Pictures exercise, 124–125
Play, 17, 38–40
    animals and, 39–40
    associative, 38
    cooperative, 38
    fantasy, 39
    intellectual, 39
    nonsocial, 38
    parallel, 38
    signals. *See* Play signals.
    solitary, 38
    structured, 39
Play signals, 81, 82–83, 96
Playfulness, 13
Practical jokes, 91–93
Pre-Halloween Day exercise. *See* Funny Costumes exercise.
Prelutsky, Jack, 141
Provine, Robert, 47, 48
Public Broadcasting Service (PBS), 34
Punning riddle, 25
Puns, 25
Puns exercise, 79

R

Racial jokes. *See* Stereotypically based humor.
Real Clown in Class exercise, 127
Relief from tension theory of humor, 15
Religious jokes. *See* Stereotypically based humor.
Report on a Comedian exercise, 132
Report on a Comedy exercise, 133
Reverse Order exercise, 79
Rhymes exercise, 74
Rhyming and nonsense, 27
Rhyming Names exercise, 73
Rickles, Don, 88
Riddles, 25
Riddles exercise, 77
Ridicule, 23
Rogers, Vincent, 117, 122
Roseanne, 13
Rovin, Jeff, 141
Ruch, Willibald, 9, 10

S

St. James, Paula, 105, 106
St. Thomas' Hospital, 6
Sawyer, Diane, 44
School, humor at. *See* Classroom, humor in the.
School Jokes Catalog exercise, 133
Schroeder, Beverly Allred, 29
Search engines, 146–147
Self-effacing humor, 109–110
    practicing, 112
Sense of humor
    advantages of having a good, 18–20
    assertiveness in, role of, 57–58

defined, 8–9
facets of, 9–10
gender and, 17–18, 28, 31
twin research study and, 6–7
See also Humor.
Sesame Street, 33, 34
Sesame Street Magazine, 150
Sex, as a humor topic, 93–94
Shaping humor, 52–53, 61–64
Share Your Blunders Game
 exercise, 130
Shared environment, 7
Shaw, George Bernard, 86
Show and Tell exercise, 125
Shrewdness, 13
Siblings, effect of, on humor
 appreciation, 54
Silly Sounds exercise, 70
Simon, Neil, 8
Sing Songs exercise, 71
Slapstick, 23–24, 27, 29
Smiles and laughter. *See* Smiling;
 Laughter.
Smiling, 40–41
 in babies, 42–43
 endogenous, 42
 exogenous, 42
Social contagion principle of
 laughter, 118
Social multiplier effect, 48
Society, effect of, on humor
 appreciation, 56–57
Solitary play, 38
Sounds and Words exercise, 130
South Park, 151
Special needs children, 103–115
 famous people who were,
 110–111

humor as a coping device for,
 108–112
humor development in, 107–108
humor studies of, 105–107
including in activities, 113
parental expectations for, 107
teaching children not to target,
 112–113
who they are, 104–105
Spontaneity, 11, 13
Spooner, Reverend W.A., 133
Spoonerisms and Oxymorons
 exercise, 133–134
Staring Contest exercise, 74
Stereotypically based humor, 94–95
Stores, as a humor resource. *See*
 Bookstores, as a humor resource;
 Magic stores, novelty shops,
 and costume shops, as a humor
 resource; Toy stores, as a humor
 resource; Video and DVD rental
 stores, as a humor resource.
Story Time exercise, 125
Strange Colors exercise, 74
Street performances, as a humor
 resource, 154
Structured play, 39
Stuber, Margaret, 44
Superiority theory of humor, the, 15,
 99
Surprise, 24, 27
Surprise the Kids exercise, 125

T

Tager-Flusberg, Helen, 105, 106
Targets, personal. *See* Personal
 targets.
Taunting, 95–96
Teasing, 95–96